JESUS CHRIST
IS RETURNING SOON

Written By

Ambassador George Spiteri

COPYRIGHTS

2025

Ambassador George Spiteri

DEDICATION

FIRST, I am writing this book to share my wisdom, my understanding, and my knowledge, which I was gifted from my God, my Father in Heaven. And as I am admonished to share my Godly gifts to all mankind, as written in 1 Peter 4:10 As each one has received a gift, minister it to one another, as good stewards of the manifold grace of God. 1 Peter 4:11 If anyone speaks, let him speak as the oracles of God. If anyone ministers, let him do it as with the ability which God supplies, that in all things God may be glorified through Jesus Christ, to whom belong the glory and the dominion forever and ever. Amen.

SECOND, I want to assure the reader that I had to prove to myself that the events that are written in the Books of the Bible did take place and did happen, as they are recorded in the Bible.

I give just two examples, which I have also recorded in this book, with two photos. One is the top of Mount Sinai, which is still burnt black from when it was on fire, at the time when the Living Creator God gave the Ten Commandments. And the other photo is that of the Blue Sapphire paving, on top of Mount Sinai, which is still there as recorded in Exodus 24:9 . Then Moses went up, also Aaron, Nadab, and Abihu, and seventy of the elders of Israel, Exodus 24:10 , and they saw the God of Israel. And there was under His feet as it were a paved work of sapphire stone, and it was blue, like the very heavens in its clarity. These two photos were given to me by two friends who climbed up Mount Sinai in Saudi Arabia.

I want to make the following clear to the readers. Jesus Christ has many different names. One is as I have already mentioned as – THE LAMB OF GOD.

For the readers to understand me, in my new book, I write His name as Jesus Christ. I am told by the Holy Scripture to write down words that my readers can understand, as written in 1 Corinthians 14:9. So likewise you, unless you utter by the tongue words easy to understand, how will it be known what is spoken? For you will be speaking into the air.

I want to share the important knowledge written in this book with the entire world. I wrote this book to introduce to every reader the True Living Creator God and His true peaceful way of life. Also, to prepare all humanity for the return of Jesus Christ, taking place in the near future.

Jesus Christ is returning to this Planet Earth in the next few years, so the waiting years for His return can be counted with the fingers of the hands, without the need of using the toes. But nobody knows the day and the hour when his feet will touch the Mount of Olives. Zechariah 14:4 And in that day His feet will stand on the Mount of Olives, which faces Jerusalem on the east. And the Mount of Olives shall be split in two, from east to west, Matthew 24:36 "But of that day and hour no one knows."

I am going to bring out things for you to read about, things that have never been heard of before.

SUMMARY OF THE BOOK

Whether you are a white or black person, or a black shaded skin person, and no matter where you live on this planet, you can trace your ancestry, all the way back for 6000 years, all the way back to Adam and Eve, because in this book I have written the two genealogies of both the white race, and also of the black race. You will also learn how the origin of the black race originated, while Adam and Eve were still alive.

You will learn how we, all humans, are conceived with the original sin of Adam and Eve. This is the reason why we all have to die, because we don't have eternal life, and the penalty of sin is DEATH, as written in Romans 6:23. For the wages of sin is death. And the reader will learn why and how Jesus Christ was conceived without the Original Sin of Adam and Eve.

In this Book, you will learn of HOW, and WHAT act Ham, the son of Noah had done, to see and discover the nakedness of his father Noah.

The reader will also learn that the Stillborn babies will be resurrected to life in the LAST DAY RESURRECTION, AND WILL BE LIVING ONE THOUSAND YEARS, ACCORDING TO THE WRITTEN WORD of the Living Creator God in the Bible.

The life of a human starts at the time of conception, at the time a male sperm penetrates and enters the female ovum.

The reader will also learn from recent discoveries how the Living Creator God preserved and saved the black race during the Flood of Noah.

I started writing this book as a short article, but my Father in Heaven kept inspiring me more and more, and it turned out to be an inspired book. This book is not mine, but I wrote it for my Father in Heaven, for His love towards all humanity, whom He loves dearly, even loving those who do not know Him.

This Book is based on the Truth. I have written this book and quoted the Bible to bring out the Truth to the reader. In this book, I have written about living a life, by the True way of life, of the Living Creator God Himself. It covers some of the history of the past 6000 years. This book explains and brings to the reader some hidden knowledge that has only now been discovered. And how the Living Creator God, have got a plan for all mankind, and it is based on an 8000 years plan, because He does not want any human to perish, as written in 2 Peter 3:8 But, beloved, do not forget this one thing, that with the Lord one day is as a thousand years, and a thousand years as one day. 2 Peter 3:9 The Lord is not slack concerning His promise, as some count slackness, but is long-suffering toward us, not willing that any should perish but that all should come to repentance. This book opens a vivid picture to the readers, helping them discern the present times in which we live, and also preparing them for the coming Tribulations ahead, in the next not-too-distant few years, before Jesus Christ returns.

I was born during WWII, and while my mother was pregnant with me, and while she was in her bedroom, 3 bombs exploded close to our farmhouse. The first bomb exploded half a mile away in the cemetery and unearthed many graves. The second bomb exploded 80 feet in front of our farmhouse, and one of its shrapnel's stuck in the limestone wall of my mother's bedroom. The shrapnel was still stuck there when I was young. And the third bomb exploded two hundred feet between two farmhouses in our street, and a man got killed.

Satan tried to kill me before I was born, a parallel like when Moses was born; Pharaoh killed all the male babies of Israel. Another parallel is when Jesus Christ was born, and Herod killed all the male children, two years and under, in Bethlehem. Matthew 2:16 Then Herod, when he saw that he was deceived by the wise men, was exceedingly angry; and he sent forth and put to death all the male children who were in Bethlehem and in all its districts, from two years old and under.

These are shrapnel holes in the wall of the cemetery Chapel, which are still there today.

Ambassador George Spiteri.

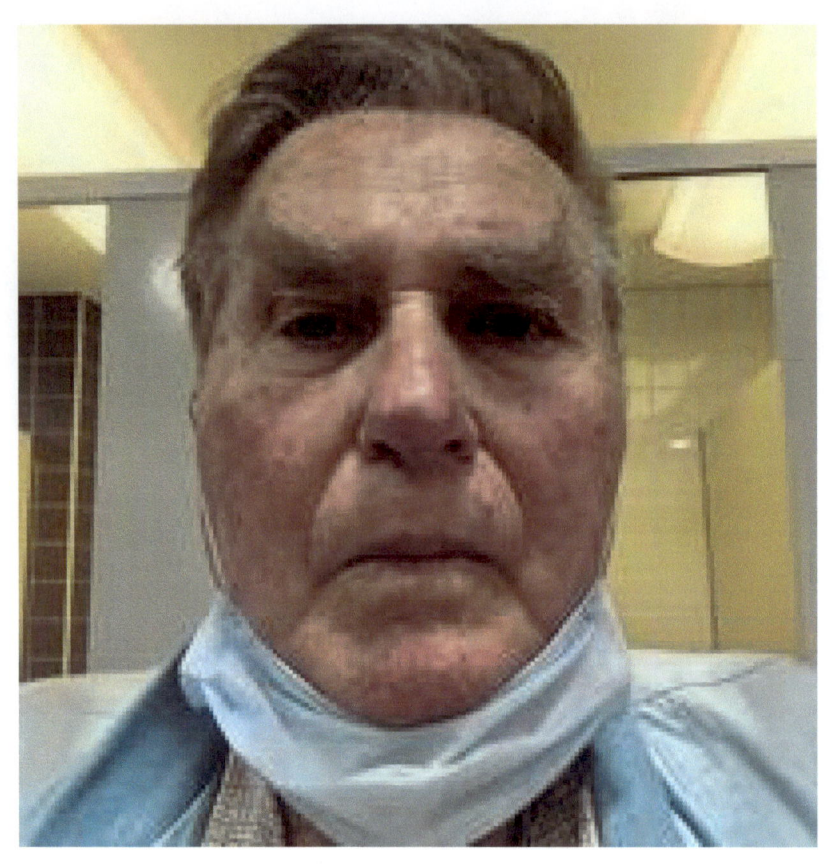

AMBASSADOR GEORGE SPITERI

ACKNOWLEDGEMENT

First and foremost, I give reverence and thanks to my Great Omnipotent Father and to my Brother Jesus Christ, who are in Heaven, for the love they have toward us humans. They love us even while we are sinners, and while we don't know them. They knew everyone of us, before their creation of the whole universe, as I have explained in this book, as written in the Scripture. I thank them for the inspiration and for helping me to write this inspired book for all mankind, because every human being has the opportunity to become a child of the Living Creator God Family. No matter what colour or what shade of your skin, you come under; the Living Creator God loves you. It is written in 1 John 4:16: 'And we have known and believed the love that God has for us.' God is love, and he who abides in love abides in God, and God in him.

May the Living Creator God in Heaven inspire you, while you are reading this book, in the same way that He has inspired me to write this book for you. Unless otherwise indicated, Bible quotations are taken from the New King James Version. Copyright 1988 by Thomas Nelson, Inc.

TABLE OF CONTENTS

This article is written based on and quoted from the True Word of the Living Creator God.

Matthew 6:24: "No one can serve two masters; for either he will hate the one and love the other, or else he will be loyal to the one and despise the other."

In other words, for someone to love and to be loyal to the Living Creator God, one has to be keeping and living by all the TEN COMMANDMENTS and not only by part of them. I will write down the TEN COMMANDMENTS a little bit later, and you can see how you compare your lifestyle, with the TEN COMMANDMENTS.

Jesus Christ said, as written in John 14:15, "If you love Me, keep My commandments."

WARNING - I would like to warn you that most of what is written here in this book, may be controversial to what **your BELIEFS** are, your **CUSTOMS**, your **CULTURES**, your **PRACTICES**, and your **TRADITIONS**, of which they may be in agreement with Satan's way of life. Reading this book may help you to repent and to change, by discarding all of the above, and to start living a new way of life, in agreement with your Living Creator God. This book will help you to make your choice.

I would also like to warn you, that there is a **SECOND LIFE** and a **SECOND DEATH,** for all those humans, as written in revelation 21:8: But the cowardly, unbelieving, abominable, murderers, sexually immoral, sorcerers, idolaters, and all liars shall have their part in the lake which burns with fire and brimstone, which is the second death."

BEWARE IF YOU ARE LIVING AS ONE OF THOSE.

The Living Creator God is the One who created Adam and Eve, and everything that was created, as written in John 1:1: In the beginning was the Word, and the Word was with God, and the Word was God. John 1:2 He was in the beginning with God. John 1:3 All things were made through Him, and without Him, nothing was made that was made. Here, the Living Creator God is called the Word.

The Living Creator God, as also is called the Word, is Jesus Christ Himself, as written in John 1:14: And the Word became flesh and dwelt among us, and we beheld His glory, the glory as of the only begotten of the Father, full of grace and truth.

Jesus Christ was also called "The Lamb of God," as written in John 1:29. The next day, John saw Jesus coming toward him and said, "Behold! The Lamb of God who takes away the sin of the world!" 1 Peter 1:19 but with the precious blood of Christ, as of **a lamb without blemish and without spot.**

The Living Creator God was without blemish and without a spot. He was **pure white,** and He created Adam and Eve in His Own image, white like Himself, as written in Genesis 1:26. Then God said, "Let Us make man in Our image, according

2

to Our likeness; let them have dominion over the fish of the sea, over the birds of the air, and over the cattle, over all the earth and over every creeping thing that creeps on the earth."

Genesis 1:27 So God created man in His own image; in the image of God, He created him; male and female He created them.

Adam and Eve produced white children after their own white images. Here I ask the question, if every living human being were white, "Where Did the Black People Come From?"

You will find the correct and true answer written a little later in this book.

I am writing this article to alert you, to make you aware, and to help you realize, to discern, and to understand, the most critical times you are living in right now, at this hour.

From Ambassador George Spiteri.

Now, I like to ask a question: If the Living Creator God Created Adam and Eve white, where did the black people come from?

This is a very intrigued question, to challenge the Creation by a very Intelligent Living Creator, God, versus Evolution. In this article, I will provide you with the true, correct, and the right answer, later in this book.

To find the correct and the true answer, we must start our research at the very beginning of human existence.

In this short article, which is evolving into a book, you will learn about, and discover knowledge of past history, that has been hidden from most of humanity, for thousands of years. Here, I will also touch on, and tell you of some future events, that will be taking place, with some of the events unfolding in your lifetime, affecting you personally, or even affecting your loved ones. If you believe, or do not believe, what you are reading here is not my business; it is left entirely up to you, if you believe it or not, or what you do. I write everything as I feel, and as I am inspired, of how things are, and how they should be. I am magnifying some of the words that proceeded from the mouth of the Living Creator God, and what the Living Creator God has already written, by His Prophets, before me.

I use the name 'The Living Creator God' in this article, to ensure that everyone reading it understands which Living Creator God I am referring to. My Father is in Heaven, because His spirit dwells in my body. My body is His temple, and I am an ambassador on this planet Earth, for both my Father and my brother Jesus Christ, as I will explain later in this short article. 2 Corinthians 5:20. Now then, we are ambassadors for Christ.1 Corinthians 3:16 Do you not know that you are the temple of God and that the Spirit of God dwells in you?

I am going to bring out things for you to read about, things that have never been heard of before. For instance, maybe you never heard that Jesus Christ is returning in the next few years, that you can count the years with your fingers of your hands. Maybe you have never heard that Jesus Christ will be grabbing Satan, and locking up Satan in prison for one thousand years. Maybe you never heard that the dead people are not living, but are asleep, and don't have a memory of anything, of what is going on while they are asleep. Even Jesus Christ said that Lazarus was asleep as written in John 11:11 These things He said, and after that He said to them, "Our friend Lazarus sleeps, but I go that I may wake him up." Even the Apostle Paul wrote that the dead are asleep as written in 1Thessallonians 4:13 But I do not want you to be ignorant, brethren, concerning those who have fallen asleep, lest you sorrow as others who have no hope.

In this article, I will disclose the origin, of The Black People. You will learn for the first time, how Satan stole the first 120 Jubilee years, to rule mankind, and Satan is ruling mankind by death, with misery, suffering, and pain, stirring up people to destroy and kill each other, making people cry, during these 120 Jubilee years. 120 Jubilee years are 120 x 49 years = 5,880 years, which are shortly coming to an end, for Satan's ruling. You will learn of an 8,000 years plan for all mankind.

You are going to read about them here, in this book. You are going to learn that 90% of this present population is going to perish, to be put to sleep, for one thousand years. And after the one thousand years of deep sleep, they, and all those who died from Adam until now, are going to wake up, to live one thousand years, to be given to them what they missed out on, during their first life, before they died their first death. During their first life, they missed out on the opportunity to have an Eternal Life.

Jesus Christ refers to this first death, as someone who is resting in a deep sleep, as written in John 11:11 as I have written earlier. John 11:12 Then His disciples said, "Lord, if he sleeps, he will get well." John 11:13 However, Jesus spoke of his death, but they thought that He was speaking about taking rest in sleep.

I ask the question: - Can you have a conversation with someone who is asleep? Do those who are asleep know what is going on around them? That's how much those who died know what is going on. They are asleep. Their spirit cannot function without a body, and their spirit soul is preserved till the time when their soul will enter a new body, to start functioning again, it is called a resurrection from their sleep. The spirit soul cannot function without a body, and the body, cannot function without a spirit soul. Those who die from Adam and Eve, until Jesus Christ returns and takes over Satan, would have lived their first life under Satan; now, and when they come back to life again, they will live one thousand years under the ruling of The Living Creator God, and after living under two different styles of life, they will be able to make a decision, about which way they choose, either die their eternal second death, never to exist again, or to have Eternal Life, living eternally with their Living Eternal God forever. Those who have died their first death cannot communicate; they are asleep, knowing nothing.

Martha, the sister of Lazarus, knew that the next time she saw her brother Lazarus, was at Lazarus's resurrection on The Last Day, meaning during the last one thousand years, of the plan of the Living Creator God, as I will explain later. John 11:23 Jesus said to her, "Your brother will rise again." John 11:24 Martha said to Him, "I know that he will rise again in the resurrection on the last day." I will write more about this last day, later on.

All this is written in this short article, based on the written Word of the Living Creator God in Heaven. This may be new knowledge for you, knowledge that you will not find anywhere else.

Some have already asked me what they have to do. You, too, may come to the stage of asking the same question, as written in Acts 2:37. Now, when they heard this, they were cut to the heart, and said to Peter and the rest of the apostles, "Men and brethren, what shall we do?"

Acts 2:38 Then Peter said to them, "Repent and let every one of you be baptized in the name of Jesus Christ, for the remission of sins, and you shall receive the gift of the Holy Spirit." Acts 2:39 For the promise is to you and to your children, and to all who are afar off, as many as the Lord our God will call.

Here the Apostle Peter is saying that baptism forgives sins, and the Holy Spirit is received after the proper baptism is performed by the individual.

The Living Creator God will give His Holy Spirit only after the correct Baptism is carried out, to those who are willing to live God's way of life, repenting from your **SINS, your BELIEFS,** your **CUSTOMS,** your **CULTURES,** your **PRACTICES**, and your **TRADITIONS**, of which they are many, and may be in agreement with Satan's way of life. Baptisms should be conducted according to the requirement of doing it, according to the set rule, as set by The Living Creator God. Jesus Christ gave us an example of how the ritual of Baptism should be carried out. We should be baptized in the same way as He was baptized. All Baptisms done differently than the Baptism of Jesus Christ, are all invalid, and the Living Creator God will not give His Holy Spirit, to those who are rebellious, to those who in their minds, think that they know better than their Creator, and they perform their baptisms, their own way, leaving The Living Creator God out of the picture.

When I was born, the very next day, they carried me to the nearest Church Building, and they poured water over my head, and they declared me baptized, and they enrolled me on the Baptism Roll of my local village. I had no idea what was going on when they poured water on my head.

If you are like me, if they poured water over your head to get you baptized, I ask you to consider and ask yourself if your Baptism is valid or not.

I only got my head wet when they poured water out of a jug over my head.

Today, I will ask the following question: Was this a valid Baptism with water poured over my head, compared to, and according to the custom and order exemplified by the same Baptism Jesus Christ received, from John the Baptist? Let us see how Jesus Christ was baptized by John. Jesus Christ did not need to be baptized because He had no sins, but He forced John the Baptist to baptize Him, to give us an example of how Baptism had to be performed and conducted, to be a valid Baptism. We find this written in the Word of God as follows.

THE BAPTISM OF JESUS CHRIST

Matthew 3:13 Then Jesus came from Galilee to John at the Jordan (River) to be baptized by him. Matthew 3:14 And John tried to prevent Him, saying, "I need to be baptized by You, and are You coming to me?"

Notice that Jesus Christ did not throw himself into the river to baptize Himself. He required John to baptize Him.

Baptism is done after an individual repents from his/her past life, of living a sinful way of life under Satan's way of life. Then burying self in the water, that all the past sins are washed away. Coming out of the water, confirms to start to live the True Living Creator God's way of life.

The moment the individual steps out of the water, the one that baptized the individual will lay hands on the head of the one who had been baptized, and ask the Living Creator God to pour out His Spirit, on the baptized individual.

And because this Baptism was done on the example of Jesus Christ, in the same manner as Jesus Christ received the Spirit of His Father, as soon as He stepped out of the water, God the Father will pour out His Spirit, into the repented baptized individual. This is the truth of the manner of BAPTISM.

John the Baptist knew that Jesus Christ had no sins to repent of and did not need to be baptized; at first, he refused to baptize Jesus Christ.

Jesus Christ wanted to be baptized, to establish the requirement and the way how Baptism had to be performed and conducted, to be a valid baptism, accompanied by repentance from our sins. Jesus Christ wanted to show us, how Baptism is to be done. A baby just two days old is not conscious and capable of repenting. Water is poured on the baby's head, without the baby's permission or willingness. Baptism is for adults only.

Matthew 3:15 But Jesus answered and said to him, "Permit it to be so now, for thus it is fitting for us to fulfill all righteousness." Then he (John) allowed Him.

Matthew 3:16 When He had been baptized, Jesus came up immediately from the water; and behold, the heavens were opened to Him, and He saw the Spirit of God descending like a dove and alighting upon Him.

Jesus Christ was baptized in the river, in deep water, and John the Baptist gave Jesus Christ a "MAJNATA" (This is a word used in my original language when swimming, and someone comes around from behind and pushes your head and your whole body underwater), meaning to dunk someone underwater. You can look up the word "MAJNATA" on Google or Wikipedia to get the full meaning, of what I am writing here.

Jesus Christ had all His body buried in the water, when He got baptized by John. And this is the proper way, in which Baptism should be done. When buried underwater, it is burying your sinful self, to start a new life style, living The Living Creator God's way

11

of life. Living by the Ten Commandments, and by what the Living Creator God requires you to live by, including celebrating His Feasts with Him.

Notice that it is written how, when Jesus Christ had been baptized, Jesus came up immediately out from the water; also, it was when He came out of the water, that His Father in Heaven poured out His Spirit on His Son, saying, as written in Matthew 3:17 And suddenly a voice came from heaven, saying, "This is My beloved Son, in whom I am well pleased." Christ's Baptism was not just pouring water on His head; He was immersed with His whole body under water.

I can freely write down and officially claim to tell you that I am the brother of Jesus Christ.

How can I claim our Brotherhood?

I will explain this to you. When I was baptized 50 years ago, in the same way and the same manner, that Jesus Christ was baptized by John the Baptist, by a MAJNATA, having my whole body being dunked under water, in the same way as Jesus Christ was baptized, to set up for us an example of how baptism has to be carried out.

When I was baptized and I came out of the water, the Living God the Father, poured out His Holy Spirit into me, and He would have said the same words, that He said to Jesus Christ "This is My beloved Son, in whom I am well pleased." At that

12

very moment, I became the brother of Jesus Christ, both of us having the same Father. Jesus Christ proves this to us when He told the Apostles to pray to His Father, as their Father in Heaven.

Jesus Christ was around 30 years of age when He got baptized, not as a baby. And it was at baptism when His Father poured out His Spirit onto Him, as written in Mark 1:10 . And immediately, coming up from the water, He saw the heavens parting and the Spirit descending upon Him like a dove.

When the correct Baptism is performed, the Living God, the Father, pours out His Spirit on the repentant individual, soon after they emerge from the water, after having been baptized. And God, my Father in Heaven, poured out His Spirit on me when I came out of the water, after I was baptized at the age of my thirtieth year of my lifetime.

As I have written in this book, my body holds the spirit from my Father in Heaven, and the Holy Scripture says that my body is His Temple, as written in   1Corinthians 3:16 . Do you not know that you are the temple of God and that the Spirit of God dwells in you? 1Corinthians 3:17 If anyone defiles the temple of God, God will destroy him. For the temple of God is holy, in which you are.

The apostles were told by Jesus Christ whom to pray to and how to pray. Jesus Christ told them to pray to their God the Father, the same Father of Jesus Christ. It makes Jesus Christ and the Apostles, to have the same Father, which makes them brothers with Jesus Christ. I claim to have Jesus Christ, as my Brother in the same way as the Apostles, as set by Jesus Christ Himself. My Brother, Jesus Christ, tells me to pray to my Father in Heaven. He doesn't tell me to make an image and pray to the image. The images are made with mouths and ears, and the images do not speak or hear. My God Father in Heaven,

I can speak to Him, and He can hear me, and He knows my needs before I even ask Him, as written in Matthew 6:8: "Therefore do not be like them. For your Father knows the things you have need of before you ask Him.

My Brother Jesus Christ, gives me the outline of how to pray to my Father, and His Father, the same Father in Heaven, as written in Matthew 6:9 . In this manner, therefore, pray: Our Father in heaven, Hallowed be Your name. Matthew 6:10 Your kingdom come. Your will be done on earth as it is in heaven. Matthew 6:11 Give us this day our daily bread. Matthew 6:12 And forgive us our debts, as we forgive our debtors. Matthew 6:13 And do not lead us into temptation, but deliver us from the evil one. (SATAN) For Yours is the kingdom and the power and the glory forever. Amen.

I ask my Father to set up his kingdom-government on this earth, and to make this earth peaceful as it is up in Heaven. Then I mention to Him my daily needs, and asked for forgiveness for all my wrongdoings. I confess my wrongdoings to Him and nobody else.

This is how I can claim that Jesus Christ, is my Brother. On Sunday afternoon, on December 23, 1990, it was my Brother Jesus Christ who came to save my life. There was nobody around who could help me, when I cut my femoral artery from behind my left knee in my left leg, by accident. I was cutting concrete with a machine all by myself, when the large cutting wheel cut me at the back of my left knee, and I was bleeding to death. I knew that I only had few minutes of life left.

Lying on my right side, and keeping my left knee as high as I could, while trying to find the artery to pinch it, and stop the bleeding, but with the artery behind my knee, I could not get it, and I knew that my life had come to an end. I was ready to give up my life. At that time I called to my Father in Heaven, and I said to Him, "I leave my spirit into your hands, but if I can be of further service to you, please keep me alive."

I had hardly finished talking to my Father, Jesus Christ came behind me, when I was lying on the ground with the blood shooting out over one foot away from me, with every heartbeat, while I was bleeding to death, prepared and ready to have my last breath. Jesus Christ, put my thumb and my finger, from my left hand, on the bleeding femur artery, to pinch the artery, to stop the profound bleeding. And when I had pinched the femur artery, Jesus Christ vanished, without letting me say thank you to him.

I started screaming for help and the neighbors called an ambulance. An ambulance came, and the paramedics bandaged my left arm to my left thigh, while I still pinched my left femur artery with my fingers. I was not far from the hospital, and the Ambulance rushed me to the hospital. They admitted me straightaway into the operating theater. While the surgeon was reconnecting my left femur artery and the vein, I died from the shock. Later when I came back, I was told that I was dead for seven and a half minutes.

My Brother Jesus Christ is the One who kept me alive, and here I am, writing this book for you at this end time, just before my Brother Jesus Christ returns from Heaven, in the same way that He was lifted up to Heaven, as written in Acts 1:10 And while they looked steadfastly toward heaven as He went up, behold, two men stood by them in white apparel, Acts 1:11 who also said, "Men of Galilee, why do you stand gazing up into heaven? This same Jesus, who was taken up from you into heaven, will so come in like manner as you saw Him go into heaven."

To this very day, every time I touch the scar behind my left knee, get reminded that my Father in Heaven accepted me to be of further service to Him, for keeping me alive, in 1990.

And as being the brother and as an Ambassador, of Jesus Christ and my Father in Heaven, I can boldly assure you that my Brother Jesus Christ is returning soon, and his feet will touch on the Mount of Olives in Jerusalem as written in Zechariah 14:4 . And in that day His feet will stand on the Mount of Olives, which faces Jerusalem on the east. And the Mount of Olives shall be split in two, from east to west, making a very large valley; Half of the mountain shall move toward the north, and half of it toward the south.

The splitting of the Mount of Olives will be the sign that My Brother Jesus Christ has returned. This is another sign, like the Azure Window in Gozo Malta, showing and giving us that the time has come, for the return of my Brother Jesus Christ, as written in this book. Zechariah 14:1 Behold, the day of the LORD is coming, And your spoil will be divided in your midst.

Zechariah 14:2 For I will gather all the nations to battle against Jerusalem; Zechariah 14:3 Then the LORD will go forth And fight against those nations, As He fights in the day of battle.

OUR HUMAN CONCEPTION

All of us humans were conceived in our mother's womb, with the original sin, passed on us from Adam and Eve. Satan's poisoned Fruit that Adam and Eve ate, is passed on every human by the male sperm of our fathers, as written in Psalms 51:5: Behold, I was brought forth in iniquity, and in sin, my mother conceived me.

How could this happen, to be sinful at our conception - at the time when a sperm from our father penetrated our mother's ovum?

I hope that all of you reading this, will understand what I am writing here.

Genesis 2:16 And the Lord God commanded the man, saying, "Of every tree of the garden you may freely eat; Genesis 2:17 but of the tree of the knowledge of good and evil you shall not eat, for in the day that you eat of it you shall surely die."

Adam and Eve disobeyed this command. They sinned, by disobeying that command, and the penalty of sin is death. Romans 6:23. For the wages of sin is death.

The fruit of this forbidden tree, had a poisonous ingredient that caused death - by separating the soul from the physical body. Satan was so clever, that he made this poisonous, deadly ingredient to penetrate the male sperm, embedding itself in the male chromosomes and releasing it into the female ovum at conception, and the newborn is poisoned to death by Satan's poison. And this is why the Holy Scripture tells us in Psalms 51:5 And in sin my mother conceived me.

Without the male sperm, no babies can be born, and every baby is conceived with this poisonous, deadly ingredient and is bound to die at some stage in life. Satan made this poisonous fruit make the Living Creator God to fail on His plan of having children with eternal life. Death on Eve was not passed on to her by a sperm, but because she directly ate the fruit and received the direct death poison from the fruit that she ate.

When Jesus Christ went to John to be baptized, John at first refused to baptize Him, because Jesus Christ had no sins to repent of, because, unlike us humans, He was conceived in His

18

mother's womb without the poisonous, deadly ingredient, because His Father was from Heaven, and for His conception, He did not have the poisonous, deadly ingredient coming from Adam.

Jesus Christ was born without the inherited sin of Adam, because His Father was not a descendant of Adam; His Father was from Heaven. According to Ron Wyatt, who claimed that he found the blood of Jesus Christ and took the blood to a laboratory in Jerusalem, the blood test result from the laboratory showed that the blood had only 24 chromosomes. 23 chromosomes were from the mother, with only one chromosome from His Father in Heaven.

Humans all have 46 chromosomes; 23 chromosomes are inherited from our mother, and 23 chromosomes are inherited from our father. We are all born with 46 chromosomes.

We humans do not have Eternal Life. To have Eternal life, we have to seek it in our present life or during our next life, of one thousand years, after a resurrection from the dead, with a new physical body of flesh and blood, living under the Government of the Living Creator God, for one thousand years without the interference of Satan, after Satan would have been destroyed forever, after the one thousand years, when Satan is released out of his prison as written in Revelation 20:2 He laid hold of the dragon, that serpent of old, who is the Devil and Satan, and bound him for a thousand years;

Revelation 20:3 and he cast him into the bottomless pit, and shut him up, and set a seal on him so that he should deceive the nations no more till the thousand years were finished. But after these things, he must be released for a little while. The living Creator God will give Satan the years that were taken away from Satan; when the Living Creator God had to shorten Satan's time, otherwise nobody would be left alive, as written in Matthew 24:22 And unless those days were shortened, no flesh would be saved; but for the elect's sake, those days will be shortened.

Satan will be released to roam again around the world promoting his disastrous way of life, as written in Revelation 20:7. Now, when the thousand years have expired, Satan will be released from his prison, Revelation 20:8, and will go out to deceive the nations which are in the four corners of the earth.

The people who had lived by The Living Creator's way of life for one thousand years, will also experience Satan's way of life, as we ourselves are experiencing it now. Then, they will be able to choose Eternal Life with The Living Creator God forever, or if they choose Satan's way of life, they will die an eternal death, and never to exist forever, like Satan and his demons. And this will be their Second Death, it means that they will be resurrected, to be destroyed forever, with a Second Death, as I will explain shortly.

It is after these one thousand years are finished that the Last Day resurrection takes place, as written in Revelation 20:5.

But the rest of the dead did not live again until the thousand years were finished.

LAST DAY: GREAT RESURRECTION.

Yes, you are reading correctly; that a second life is prepared for all those who died from Adam to those who die before Jesus Christ returns, as written in Revelation 20:12: "And I saw the dead, small and great, standing before God, and the books were opened." And another book was opened, which is the Book of Life. And the dead were judged according to their works, by the things which were written in the books.

Revelation 20:13 The sea gave up the dead who were in it, and Death and Hades (The Graves) delivered up the dead who were in them. And they were judged, each one according to his works. I like to say to the reader, that those who were resurrected were not instantly judged, but the scripture tells us that they were judged according to how they conducted their lives, meaning they had to live some period of time, before they were finally judged, of how they lived.

The books of the written Words of The Living Creator God, will be open for all of them to understand their writings, and they will learn to live, according to the requirements of what is written in them. Then, they will be judged according to how they lived in accordance with the written books.

Those who take part in this Last Day resurrection will live one thousand years. This is based on one day, meaning one thousand years. This will be the eighth and the last one thousand years (millennium) in the plan of the Living Creator God's plan for all mankind. 2 Peter 3:8 But, beloved, do not forget this one thing, that with the Lord one day is as a thousand years and a thousand years as one day. Psalms 90:4 For a thousand years in Your sight Are like yesterday when it is past and like a watch in the night. As I have written earlier, Martha called these last one thousand years, "THE LAST DAY."

Yes, they will be living a second life of one thousand years. Ecclesiastes 6:3 "If a man begets a hundred children and lives many years, so that the days of his years are many, but his soul is not satisfied with goodness, or indeed he has no burial, I say that a stillborn child is better than he—"

A stillborn child is better than he, because the stillborn child did not go to the trouble of a first life living many years, under Satan, like him, and the stillborn child will enjoy its life in this Last Day resurrection and live one thousand years, under the True Living God way of life.

The stillborn child has never seen the sun or known anything, as written in Ecclesiastes 6:5. Though it has not seen the sun or known anything, this stillborn child is better off because it did not suffer under Satan like the one who lived one thousand years twice. Ecclesiastes 6:6.

Could it be possible that some humans are going to be living a thousand years twice? Yes it is possible. Starting with

Adam, he lived 930 years, as written in Genesis 5:5 So all the days that Adam lived were nine hundred and thirty years; and he died.

We also have recorded Genesis 5:20 So all the days of Jared were nine hundred and sixty-two years; and he died. And we have the longest lifelong recorded as written in Genesis 5:27 So all the days of Methuselah were nine hundred and sixty-nine years; and he died.

From what I understand, those who have lived a thousand years twice, lived in two different periods of time. The first one thousand years short, in the period of time from Adam to the time when Jesus Christ returns. The second life of one thousand years will be on the eight day, one thousand years period of time.

From what we just read, I have come to the conclusion that there is a one-thousand-year life period, during the eight thousand years, represented by one day, the Holy eight day after the seven days of the feast of Tabernacles. And also came to the conclusion that stillborn children, including those children that have been aborted before they saw the sun, will be resurrected, and will be included in this, one thousand year period.

This is my understanding according to what is written in Ecclesiastes.

Now I write again, the following verse of Revelation 20:12: "And I saw the dead, small and great, standing before God, and the books were opened." And another book was opened, which is the Book of Life. And the dead were judged according to their works, by the things which were written in the books. It says SMALL, those that were aborted, and the Stillborn. The GREAT are those who had lived under Satan.

All those who will refuse to live by the written Words of the Living Creator God will die their Second Death, never to exist anymore forever, as written in Revelation 20:14. Then Death and Hades were cast into the lake of fire. This is the second death. Revelation 20:15 And anyone not found written in the Book of Life was cast into the lake of fire.

All of us from Adam to all those who die before Jesus Christ returns, would have lived under the burden of Satan, in misery, wars, death, sickness, diseases, and all sorts of sufferings. On the Last Day of Resurrection, those resurrected will come back to life with a new, flesh-and-blood body in a totally different environment, and they will live under the way of life, as established by the Living Creator God, in a world governed by the Creator's government.

KEY TO THE DOOR THAT LEADS TO ETERNAL LIFE

I will also tell you, what Jesus Christ told the one who asked the question about what he had to do, to have eternal life. He knew that he did not possess eternal life. Please understand the answer that Jesus Christ gave to that question.

Matthew 19:16 Now behold, one came and said to Him, "Good Teacher, what good thing shall I do that I may have eternal life?"

Matthew 19:17 So He said to him, "Why do you call Me good? No one is good but one, that is, God. But if you want to enter into life, keep the commandments."

Matthew 19:18 He said to Him, "Which ones?" Jesus said, "'You Shall Not Murder,' 'You Shall Not Commit Adultery,' 'You Shall Not Steal,' 'You Shall Not Bear False Witness.'"

Matthew 19:19 "Honor Your Father and Your Mother," And "You Shall Love Your Neighbor as Yourself."

Jesus Christ referred to and quoted from the TEN COMMANDMENTS.

The **TEN COMMANDMENTS are** the key to lead us towards **ETERNAL LIFE**.

We don't have eternal life, and by living by the Ten Commandments, as written by the Living Creator God Himself on Mount Sinai, is the first step that will lead us to achieving Eternal life. When the Living Creator God descended on Mount Sinai, the whole mountain was on fire, and the rocks got burned black as the photo below. And here I will insert a photo taken recently, with the top of Mount Sinai in Saudi Arabia, which is still burnt black at the top. It is a confirmation that what we have in the written Word of the Living Creator God, that this event did take place and it is true.

This is a photo of Mount Sinai; it still bears the scars of fire from Saudi Arabia. Galatians 4:25. For this, Hagar is Mount Sinai in Arabia.

Exodus 19:18 Now Mount Sinai was completely in smoke because the Lord descended upon it in fire. Its smoke ascended like the smoke of a furnace, and the whole mountain quaked greatly.

Exodus 24:17 The sight of the glory of the LORD was like a consuming fire, on the top of the mountain, in the eyes of the children of Israel.

Deuteronomy 5:3 The Lord did not make this covenant only with our fathers, but with us also, those who are here today, all of us who are alive.

Deuteronomy 5:4 The Lord talked with you face to face on the mountain from the midst of the fire.

Deuteronomy 5:22 "These words the Lord spoke to all your assembly, in the mountain from the midst of the fire, the cloud, and the thick darkness, with a loud voice, and He added no more. And He wrote them on two tablets of stone and gave them to me."

When Moses went up on Mount Sinai, the living Creator God was standing on a pavement of blue sapphires, as written in Exodus 24:9. Then Moses went up, also Aaron, Nadab, and Abihu, and seventy of the elders of Israel (Exodus 24:10), and they saw the God of Israel. And there was under His feet, as it were, a paved work of sapphire stones, and it was like the very color of the sky in its clarity.

The Sapphires stone pavement is still visible on the mountain, and a friend gave me this photo after he visited the top of the mountain and came across the sapphire pavement.

Friends that climbed on Mount Sinai gave me these photos.

THE TEN COMMANDMENTS AS WRITTEN BY GOD'S FINGER

Jesus Christ said in Matthew 19:17, "If you want to enter life, keep the commandments." This is one of the required actions needed.

Jesus Christ also said, as written in John 14:15, "If you love Me, keep My commandments."

Exodus 20:1 "And God spoke all these words, saying: 2 "I am the Lord your God, who brought you out of the land of Egypt, out of the house of bondage."

1st Commandment: - Exodus 20:3 "You shall have no other gods before me."

2nd Commandment: - Exodus 20:4 "You shall not make for yourself a carved image--any likeness of anything that is in heaven above, or that is in the earth beneath, or that is in the water under the earth; 5 you shall not bow down to them nor serve them. For I, the Lord your God, am a jealous God, visiting the iniquity of the fathers upon the children to the third and fourth generations of those who hate Me, 6 but showing mercy to thousands, to those who love Me and keep My commandments."

3rd Commandment: - Exodus 20:7 "You shall not take the name of the Lord your God in vain, for the

Lord will not hold him guiltless who takes His name in vain."

4th Commandment: Exodus 20:9 Six days you shall labor and do all your work, Exodus 20:10 but the seventh day is the Sabbath of the Lord your God. In it you shall do no work: you, nor your son, nor your daughter, nor your male servant, nor your female servant, nor your cattle, nor your stranger who is within your gates. Exodus 20:11 Forin six days the Lord made the heavens and the earth, the sea, and all that is in them, and rested the seventh day. Therefore, the Lord blessed the Sabbath day and hallowed it.

5th Commandment: - Exodus 20:12 "Honour your father and your mother, that your days may be long upon the land which the Lord your God is giving you."

6th Commandment: - Exodus 20:13 "You shall not murder."

7th Commandment: - Exodus 20:14 "You shall not commit adultery."

8th Commandment: - Exodus 20:15 "You shall not steal."

9th Commandment: - Exodus 20:16 "You shall not bear false witness against your neighbor."

32

10th Commandment: - Exodus 20:17 "You shall not covet your neighbor's house; you shall not covet your neighbor's wife, nor his male servant, nor his female servant, nor his ox, nor his donkey, nor anything that is your neighbor's."

These are the Ten Commandments, that were written by the finger of the Living Creator God and, as quoted by Jesus Christ, written on two tablets of stone as written in Deuteronomy 9:10. Then the Lord delivered to me two tablets of stone written with the finger of God, and on them were all the words which the Lord had spoken to you on the mountain from the midst of the fire in the day of the assembly.

Revelation 22:14 Blessed are those who do His commandments, that **they may have the right to the tree of life.** Without living by all the Ten Commandments, one cannot have access to acquire Eternal Life. The Ten Commandments are the Key to lead to the Eternal Life.

As I have written earlier, the Ten Commandments are the KEY, and who have a key, have the right to unlock the DOOR. I will write more about this DOOR later on in this book.

ARE YOU DECEIVED BY SATAN, AND SATAN IS YOUR MASTER?

ARE YOU WORSHIPPING SATAN, AND NOT KNOWING IT?

The Scripture says that Satan has deceived the whole world. Revelation 12:9: that serpent of old, called the Devil and Satan, who deceives the whole world;

Those who are not living by the laws of the Living Creator God, and they say that they are not deceived by Satan, are saying that the Living Creator God is a liar, for He wrote that about Satan. This is the same scenario; Satan told Eve in the Garden of Eden, that her Creator is a liar.

The Living Creator God has written the TEN COMMANDMENTS with His own finger, as written in Exodus 31:18: He gave Moses two tablets of the Testimony, tablets of stone, written with the finger of God. When Jesus Christ returns, He will be ruling this planet with the TEN COMMANDMENTS. Do you think that people will welcome Jesus Christ with open arms? They will reject Him, and they will make war against Him in the valley of Armageddon, as written in Revelation 17:12 "The ten horns which you saw are ten kings, who have received no kingdom as yet., Revelation 17:14 These will make war with the Lamb, and the Lamb will overcome them, for He is Lord of Lords and King of kings.

All those who profess to be Christians, and say that they are followers of Jesus Christ, ought to live in the same lifestyle, that Jesus Christ lived, by following His example, as written in 1 Peter 2:21. Christ also suffered for us, leaving us an example that you should follow in His steps.

Jesus Christ had his life focused on all the TEN COMMANDMENTS, not keeping some and ignoring others. Most professed Christians ignore, and do not live by some of the TEN COMMANDMENTS, and I am going to mention just two of the main ones. Some Christians ignore and do not keep, or obey the 2nd Commandment: - Exodus 20:4 "You shall not make for yourself a carved image—any likeness of anything that is in heaven above, or that is in the earth beneath, or that is in the water under the earth; 5 you shall not bow down to them nor serve them. 4th Commandment: - Exodus 20:8 "Remember the Sabbath day, to keep it holy. 9 Six days you shall labour and do all your work, 10 but the seventh day is the Sabbath of the Lord your God.

The Scripture says, that when one breaks only one of the TEN COMMANDMENTS, that individual is guilty of all the TEN COMMANDMENTS, as written by the Apostle James in James 2:10. For whoever shall keep the whole law and yet stumble in one point, he is guilty of all. I have written something for you, to think about before you give the answer: that you are not deceived by Satan, and that Satan is not your master, and that you are not his servant.

When Jesus Christ returns, He will be ruling this earth with the TEN COMMANDMENTS. The people who will be left alive, will carry their baggage of **Beliefs, Customs, Cultures, Practices, and Traditions,** with them. At first, they will be stubborn about discarding their baggage, and starting to obey Jesus Christ, living the way of life according to the Living Creator God. And the scripture says that those who will not obey Jesus Christ, as written in Revelation 2:27, 'He Shall Rule Them with A Rod of Iron; They Shall Be Dashed to Pieces Like the Potter's Vessels'—as I also have received from My Father; Revelation 19:15. Now out of His mouth goes a sharp sword, that with it He should strike the nations. And He Himself will rule them with a rod of iron. He Himself treads the winepress of the fierceness and wrath of Almighty God.

By ruling by the Ten Commandments, there will be peace, on earth, because will love their neighbor like themselves.

Revelation 19:16 And He has on His robe and on His thigh a name written: King of Kings, and Lord of Lords. Jesus Christ will be ruling this entire planet from Jerusalem.

If some of the nations that are left alive, refuse to obey Jesus Christ, and to keep and celebrate the Living Creator God's Holy Feasts, it is written in Zechariah 14:16, And it shall come to pass that everyone who is left of all the nations which came against Jerusalem shall go up from year to year to worship the King, the Lord of hosts, and to keep the Feast of Tabernacles.

Zechariah 14:17 And it shall be that whichever of the families of the earth do not come up to Jerusalem to worship the King, the Lord of hosts, on them there will be no rain.

Zechariah 14:18 If the family of Egypt will not come up and enter in, they shall have no rain; they shall receive the plague with which the Lord strikes the nations who do not come up to keep the Feast of Tabernacles.

Zechariah 14:19 This shall be the punishment of Egypt and the punishment of all the nations that do not come up to keep the Feast of Tabernacles.

The Living Creator God, celebrates His Holy Feasts Annually. And He wants us humans to celebrate with Him His Holy Feasts, as written in Leviticus 23:2 "Speak to the children of Israel, and say to them: 'The feasts of the LORD, which you shall proclaim to be holy convocations, these are My feasts. Leviticus 23:3 'Six days shall work be done, but the seventh day is a Sabbath of solemn rest, a holy convocation. You shall do no work on it; it is the Sabbath of the LORD in all your dwellings.

After some time, the entire world will be seeking to live the Living Creator God's way of life.

As an ambassador of the coming Government of the Living Creator God, I can tell you that when Jesus Christ returns, after getting rid of Satan, He will establish the Government of the

Living Creator God and rule this earth with the TEN COMMANDMENTS. The TEN COMMANDMENTS will create peace on this earth, because all those who obey and live by these TEN COMMANDMENTS will be loving their Living Creator God and loving their fellow humans as themselves. Everyone will be living in peace and harmony, in love, and they will not learn war anymore, as written in Isaiah 2:4. He shall judge between the nations and rebuke many people; they shall beat their swords into plowshares and their spears into pruning hooks; nation shall not lift up sword against nation, neither shall they learn war anymore.

When the coming government of the Living Creator God is established here on this planet earth, people will be seeking to learn the Living Creator God's way of life, as written in Isaiah 2:3. Many people shall come and say, "Come, and let us go up to the mountain of the Lord, to the house of the God of Jacob; He will teach us His ways, and we shall walk in His paths." For out of Zion shall go forth the law, and the word of the Lord from Jerusalem.

The coming government of the Living Creator God will have its headquarters in Jerusalem. As an ambassador of the coming government of the Living Creator God, I can write down that this is real and true, friends. What you are reading here are not my words, but the words that the Living Creator God wants you to read and to hear. What I wrote here may touch your heart, and you may reject everything I've written. This is important, and

I will write it again. If only one commandment is not kept, it is breaking all the TEN COMMANDMENTS, as written in James 2:10. For whoever shall keep the whole law and yet stumble in one point, he is guilty of all.

Living by these Ten Commandments is the key to the door that leads to receiving eternal life. Without living by these Ten Commandments, people are living contrary to the Living Creator God, and according to the second commandment, it says that you hate the Living Creator God.

The Lamb of God = John 1:2. He was in the beginning with God. John 1:3 All things were made through Him, and without Him nothing was made that was made.

John 1:12 But as many as received Him, to them He gave the right to become children of God, to those who believe in His name:

John 1:14 And the Word (LAMB) became flesh and dwelt among us, and we beheld His glory, the glory as of the only begotten of the Father, full of grace and truth.

The LAMB of God was white, and He created His sheep white, in His image.

Genesis 1:27 So God created man in His own image; in the image of God, He created him; male and female He created them.

John 1:29 The next day John saw Jesus coming toward him and said, "Behold! The Lamb of God who takes away the sin of the world!"

The black sheep appeared on the world scene many years after the creation of Adam and Eve, when the world was becoming well populated, as I have researched and proven to myself, and I have recorded it here in this book, written in simple language, for you to understand.

Adam and Eve were not created with eternal life, and humans are not born with it either. If we want to receive eternal life in this first life, we have to seek it earnestly; otherwise, we will die and be resurrected with a new body of flesh and blood, as mentioned earlier. And in our second life, it will be much easier to obtain eternal life, because Satan will be gone forever, as I will write later on.

Adam and Eve, when they disobeyed their Living Creator God, they were forbidden to eat from the tree that would have given them eternal life. As I will write later in this book, they were also forbidden to have access to the tree that would have given them eternal life. Genesis 3:22 And now, lest he put out his hand and take also of the tree of life and eat and live forever." Genesis 3:24 So He drove out the man, and He placed cherubim at the east of the garden of Eden and a flaming sword which turned every way to guard the way to the tree of life.

The Living Creator God blocked, and shut the doorway for humans to have access to eternal life, and the Living Creator God Himself became the locked door, to the way leading to receiving eternal life. Jesus Christ gave us the key to open the locked door, which leads to the way of having eternal life. When he said that, to receive eternal life is to keep and to live by the TEN COMMANDMENTS.

Jesus Christ said that He is that door. As written in John 10:7, Jesus said to them again, "Most assuredly, I say to you, I am the door of the sheep." John 10:9: I am the door. If anyone enters by me, he will be saved and will go in and out and find pasture.

From this book, you will learn many new discoveries, from the written true word of the living Creator God. The Creator God has provided for us His written books, for us humans,

41

because He wants to communicate with us. He wants us to have a happy life, even while living under the burden of Satan.

MOST PEOPLE ON THIS ENTIRE PLANET ARE LIVING WITH SATAN'S LIES

You are also going to learn how the Living Creator God, was the One who became Jesus Christ, and He has a plan set out for eight thousand years, of dealing with mankind. And how each of the one thousand years, is represented by one day, and one day represents each one thousand years, of the Living Creator God.

You will also learn why, the ship on which the Apostle Paul was chained as a prisoner, while he was en route to Rome, had to be destroyed by the Living Creator God, so that Paul could carry out part of the plan, of the Living Creator God regarding the Maltese Islands. We are now living at the end of the six thousand years since the creation of Adam.

After Satan, the ruler of this world, is locked up for one thousand years, Jesus Christ will replace Satan, and Jesus Christ will be the ruler of this earth, together with His saints. Jesus Christ will be ruling this earth with the TEN COMMANDMENTS, and there will be peace and harmony among the people.

The next, seventh, one thousand years, that will be starting very soon, in a matter of a few more years from now, are represented with the weekly Holy day of Saturday, which is the seventh day of the week. It is also represented by seven days of

God's annual Feast Day of Tabernacles. Found written in Leviticus 23:33.

The eight thousand years in the Living Creator God's plan, are represented by God's annual Holy Feast Day, also called the eight day, and the Last Great Day. All of this is explained in the short article, which I am writing here. Found written in Leviticus 23:36. This Last Great Day - I also figure it as the Last One Thousand Years, in the plan of the Living Creator God, based on as for God one day is one thousand years, as written in Psalms 90:4 For a thousand years in Your sight Are like yesterday when it is past, And like a watch in the night. One Day. We also find it written in 2 Peter 3:8 But, beloved, do not forget this one thing, that with the Lord one day is as a thousand years, and a thousand years as one day.

The Eight Day Holy Feast of rest, is again mentioned in Leviticus 23:39 'Also on the fifteenth day of the seventh month, when you have gathered in the fruit of the land, you shall keep the feast of the LORD for seven days; on the first day there shall be a Sabbath-rest, and on **the eighth day a Sabbath-rest.**

The Living Creator God made humans on his very own image, as written in Genesis 1:26 Then God said, "Let Us make man in Our image, according to Our likeness; let them have dominion over the fish of the sea, over the birds of the air, and over the cattle, over all the earth and over every creeping thing that creeps on the earth."

God gave Adam and Eve His whole creation, of this planet to rule it for six thousand years, under their Living Creator God. The six thousand years are represented with the work and activities of the first six days of the week, but unfortunately Adam and Eve, choose Satan to rule over them, and rejected their Living Creator God, and in doing so, Satan replaced their Living Creator God, and Satan became the god of this world, as written in 2 Corinthians 4:4 whose minds the god of this age has blinded, who do not believe, Satan's fruit is death and a misery life, with wars, diseases, pain, and famine, ending with death, under Satan's rule of six thousand years.

Adam was created to become a split image of his Living Creator God, in every way. The Living Creator God created Adam and Eve for life, and not to death. The Tree that gave Eternal Life was there in the Garden for them, but they never tasted it, which would have given them eternal life, as written in Genesis 2:9. And out of the ground the LORD God made every tree grow that is pleasant to the sight and good for food. The tree of life was also in the midst of the garden, and the tree of the knowledge of good and evil.

The Living Creator God protected the Tree that gave Eternal life that no human being will have access to it, as written in Genesis 3:24 So He drove out the man; and He placed cherubim at the east of the garden of Eden, and a flaming sword which turned every way, to guard the way to the tree of life.

Death came on Adam and Eve, from Satan, and not from the Living Creator God. The Living Creator God gives life, and in contrast, Satan gives death. The Living Creator God made Adam and Eve to have a free choice of thinking and of choosing. The Living Creator God, gave Adam and Eve their choice: to choose ETERNAL LIFE by eating from the Tree of Life, or death by eating from Satan's tree that gives DEATH. The Living Creator, has set before us ETERNAL LIFE, or ETERNAL DEATH, He wants us to choose the ETERNAL LIFE, as written in Deuteronomy 30:19 I call heaven and earth as witnesses today against you, that I have set before you life and death, blessing and cursing; therefore, choose life, that both you and your descendants may live;

We don't have Eternal Life, and to have Eternal Life, we still have to choose it.

The Living Creator God warned Adam and Eve, that there in the Garden, which the Living Creator God gave them to eat from all the trees, there also was a dangerous tree, that if they eat the fruit of it, they will die, as written in Genesis 2:16 And the LORD God commanded the man, saying, "Of every tree of the garden you may freely eat; Genesis 2:17 but of the tree of the knowledge of good and evil, you shall not eat, for in the day that you eat of it you shall surely die." Adam and Eve disobeyed their Living Creator God, and unfortunately, Adam and Eve, they chose death.

The Living Creator God, didn't plant the tree of death, because God is Good as written in Psalms 73:1 A Psalm of Asaph. Truly God is good.

The Living Creator God gave Adam and Eve, His whole garden, which He planted for them, free to eat from, except from one poisonous tree, that belonged to Satan. God planted the garden to supply and to provide free food for humanity. It was Satan who planted his poisonous tree in God's Garden. The Living Creator God warned them about the consequences, if they ate from Satan's fruit.

In the same garden, God also had planted His Tree of Life, from the fruit of which gave eternal life, to those who ate from it, with the same level of life that the Living Creator God Himself possessed. Genesis 2:9 And out of the ground the LORD God made every tree grow that is pleasant to the sight and good for food. The tree of life was also in the midst of the garden, and the tree of the knowledge of good and evil.

After Adam and Eve ate the fruit from Satan's tree, the Creator God protected the Tree of Life, as written in Genesis 3:22. Then the LORD God said, "Behold, the man has become like one of Us, to know good and evil. And now, lest he put out his hand and take also of the tree of life, and eat, and live forever."—

Genesis 3:23 Therefore, the LORD God sent him out of the garden of Eden, to till the ground from which he was taken. Genesis 3:24 So He drove out the man; and He placed cherubim at the east of the garden of Eden, and a flaming sword which turned every way, to guard the way to the tree of life. We humans, without the fruit from the Tree of Life, don't have eternal life. God kicked Adam and Eve out of His garden, and made them to provide for themselves. And we, present-day humans, also have to provide our own food to survive.

Satan knows how to promote and how to sell his products by lying, even to this very day. Satan himself lured Eve to his tree, and with too much talking to Eve, Satan convinced Eve, that their Creator God lied to them, about the fruit from his tree. Genesis 3:1 Now the serpent was more cunning than any beast of the field which the LORD God had made. And he said to the woman, "Has God indeed said, 'You shall not eat of every tree of the garden'?" Genesis 3:2 And the woman said to the serpent, "We may eat the fruit of the trees of the garden; Genesis 3:3 But of the fruit of the tree which is in the midst of the garden, God has said, 'You shall not eat it, nor shall you touch it, lest you die." Did you catch that? Satan planted his poisonous tree in the middle of the Living Creator's garden.

This verse of Genesis 3:3 shows us that Eve was a distance away from Satan's tree, and it was Satan who chased Eve, to promote the fruit of his tree to her. While talking to her, Satan walked her to his poisonous tree. Eve did not realize that Satan was leading her to his poisonous tree. To this very day, people do not realize how Satan is leading them to destruction. Satan twisted the Living Creator God's words, and Satan lied to Eve about the results of eating the fruit of Satan's tree. Satan still twists and lies, about the words of the Living Creator God to this very day. This is why Jesus Christ referred to Satan as a liar, from the very beginning, as written in John 8:44 You are of your father the devil, and the desires of your father you want to do. He was a murderer from the beginning, and does not stand in the truth, because there is no truth in him. When he speaks a lie, he speaks from his own resources, for he is a liar and the father of it. Jesus Christ said that Satan was a murderer from the beginning, because Satan gave the poison of death to Adam and Eve, and to every human to this very day, Satan is still killing us all.

Adam and Eve were not created with eternal life; they had to choose to have eternal life. Unfortunately, Adam and Eve chose death instead of eternal life, when they ate the poisonous fruit of Satan. Adam and Eve did not eat from the tree of Life, which would have given them eternal life. God does not force any human to choose what to do. Every human has a free moral freedom to make his or her own choices and decisions. Adam and Eve could have chosen to eat the fruit from the Tree of Life, which also was there in the garden for them, to eat from, and it would have given them eternal life, of the same level of their Living Creator God, and lived forever, as written in Genesis 3:22 Then the LORD God said, "Behold, the man has become like one of Us, to know good and evil. And now, lest he put out his hand and take also of the tree of life, and eat, and live forever."

This verse confirms that we humans do not possess or have eternal life within us. WE receive death from the poison that Adam and Eve ate. Satan was so clever that he made the results of his poison contagious, capable of spreading like a virus, that can pass on from one generation to the next generation, affecting all of us humans.

Satan has filled up this earth with his lies, about people going to Heaven and to hell, to burn, and living there forever in those places. This is the biggest blatant lie, Satan comes out with. The spirit, the soul, in our body, is the real being in us, using the physical body to function. When we die, we leave our body that we were using its parts, to do what we desired to do, while we were in it, and when we come out of our body, that body becomes useless, and also we, our spirit, the soul, that functions inside our physical body, also become useless outside of our bodies, even our memory is not there anymore, as it is written in Ecclesiastes 9:5 For the living know that they will die; But the dead know nothing, And they have no more reward, For the memory of them is forgotten.

When we die, we, our spirit, our soul, our real self, when we come out from our body, and we leave our body behind, we, the self, the spirit, the soul, is preserved by God The Father, for a future resurrection, when we, our spirit, our soul is entered into another new body, a natural body like the first body, that we already had, in our first life. Or the second choice we may

50

resurrect with a spiritual immortal, uncorrupted body, by a resurrection. Without a body, our spirit, our soul, we are asleep, and as a spirit, as a soul, we cannot function without a body.

The real Jesus Christ was the spirit-soul, functioning within His human body. And before He died, He asked His Father to take care of him - His soul, His spirit, because He knew that His spirit, His soul would not function, when His spirit, His soul, the real Self Jesus Christ, left His body, as written in Luke 23:46 And when Jesus had cried out with a loud voice, He said, "Father, 'INTO YOUR HANDS I COMMIT MY SPIRIT.'" Having said this, He breathed His last.

When Jesus Christ got Baptized by John, Jesus Christ received another spirit - soul, from his Father in Heaven, as written in Matthew 3:16 When He had been baptized, Jesus came up immediately from the water; and behold, the heavens were opened to Him, and He saw the Spirit of God descending like a dove and alighting upon Him.

Matthew 3:17 And suddenly a voice came from heaven, saying, "This is My beloved Son, in whom I am well pleased." Matthew 12:17 that it might be fulfilled which was spoken by Isaiah the prophet, saying:

Matthew 12:18 "BEHOLD! MY SERVANT WHOM I HAVE CHOSEN, MY BELOVED IN WHOM MY SOUL IS WELL PLEASED! I WILL PUT MY SPIRIT UPON HIM, AND HE WILL DECLARE JUSTICE TO THE GENTILES.

While Jesus Christ was about to die, while hanging on the stake, felt that His father forsook Him, as written in Matthew 27:46 And about the ninth hour Jesus cried out with a loud voice, saying, "Eli, Eli, lama sabachthani?" that is, "MY GOD, MY GOD, WHY HAVE YOU FORSAKEN ME?"

Some historians say that at that moment Jesus Christ took on Himself all the sins of the entire world on Himself, to pay for all humans penalties of death. And being loaded with our sins, God The Father had to leave His Son, because of our sins, on Jesus Christ shoulders. Jesus Christ was killed as a sacrifice sin offering, the real Lamb of God, who wiped out the world sins as written in, Joh 1:29 The next day John saw Jesus coming toward him, and said, **"Behold! The Lamb of God who takes away the sin of the world!**

Jesus Christ had no sins, and by being killed He paid our penalties of death in our stead.

The same spirit from God the Father, that entered into Jesus Christ, also entered into all those saints, who were gathered together on the day of Pentecost, as written in Acts 2:1.When the Day of Pentecost had fully come, they were all with one accord in one place. Acts 2:2 And suddenly there came a sound from heaven, as of a rushing mighty wind, and it filled the whole house where they were sitting. Acts 2:3 Then there appeared to them divided tongues, as of fire, and one sat upon each of them.

Acts 2:4 And they were all filled with the Holy Spirit and began to speak with other tongues, as the Spirit gave them utterance. These saints received God's Spirit as fire over their heads. These saints passed on the Spirit of God, which was in them, by laying their hands on the heads of those who got baptized, as written in Acts 8:17. Then they laid hands on them, and they received the Holy Spirit. Acts 8:18 And when Simon saw that through the laying on of the apostles' hands the Holy Spirit was given, he offered them money.

The Spirit of the Living Creator God spreads like fire, as when fire from one candle lights up another candle, and all the candles receive the same fire of the original candle. This same Spirit of the Living Creator God is still available around the world, and it is passed on to others from those who have the Spirit of the Living Creator God within themselves, by placing their hands upon the heads of those who have just been baptized, in the right manner, as I have written earlier in this book..

Very likely, those saints who were gathered together at Pentecost, were already baptized by John the Baptist, as written in Mark 1:4: John came baptizing in the wilderness and preaching a baptism of repentance for the remission of sins. Mark 1:5 Then all the land of Judea, and those from Jerusalem, went out to him and were all baptized by him in the Jordan River, confessing their sins.

Did you notice what you just read, "A BAPTISM OF REPENTANCE FOR THE REMISSION OF SINS." In other words, how could a two day old baby, being baptized, repent from its sins?

The Living Creator's Spirit is always given immediately after the proper Baptism. The living chosen saints, also receive this extra spirit from God the Father, when they receive the correct, and the real Baptism, the same Baptism received by Jesus Christ, when John immersed Jesus Christ whole, His entire body under water, as written in Acts 8:12 But when they believed Philip as he preached the things concerning the kingdom of God, and the name of Jesus Christ, both men and women were baptized. Acts 8:14 Now when the apostles who were at Jerusalem heard that Samaria had received the word of God, they sent Peter and John to them.

Acts 8:15 who, when they had come down, prayed for them that they might receive the Holy Spirit. Acts 8:16 For as yet He had fallen upon none of them. They had only been baptized in the name of the Lord Jesus. Acts 8:17 Then they laid hands on them, and they received the Holy Spirit. The Holy Spirit is passed on from the one who is already filled by the Holy Spirit, and passes it on by placing their BAPTISM AND THE SPIRIT OF MY FATHER GOD hands upon the head of the one who has just been baptized.

It is after the real baptism, that God the Father sends His Spirit into the baptized human. This extra spirit, which God the Father gives to His chosen saints, helps the saints to live God's way of life, in this present confused world, ruled by Satan. It is impossible to live God's way of life under Satan, without the help of God's Spirit.

The living saints have this spirit from God the Father in them, and it is this spirit within them that produces the immortal, incorruptible body to live forever, as written in Romans 8:9. But you are not in the flesh but in the Spirit, if indeed the Spirit of God dwells in you. Now if anyone does not have the Spirit of Christ, he is not His. Romans 8:11 But if the Spirit of Him who raised Jesus from the dead dwells in you, He who raised Christ from the dead will also give life to your mortal bodies through His Spirit who dwells in you.

And this is how Eternal Life, to live forever comes in. Our mortal bodies need this extra Spirit to obtain ETERNAL LIFE. From this verse of Romans 8:11, we learn that it is the Spirit given from the Father that will rise up the saints into spiritual bodies, to live forever in the Family of the Living Creator God. The living saints are the living temple of the Living Creator God, as written in 1 Corinthians 3:16. Do you not know that you are the temple of God and that the Spirit of God dwells in you? 1 Corinthians 3:17 If anyone defiles the temple of God, God will destroy him. For the temple of God is holy, in which you are.

From the written TRUE Word of God, those chosen saints by God the Father need to be properly Baptized, and have other elder saints lay their hands over their heads, asking God the Father to send His Spirit to dwell in the new saints. This is very clear for everyone to understand this procedure. And it is this extra spirit, that comes from God the Father, which enters the saints, which will give them the same resurrection that Jesus Christ had, resurrecting with a spirit body. Without the spirit from God the Father, only a physical flesh and blood body can be resurrected, as I will explain later in this book. Jesus Christ resurrected with a spirit body, because He had the spirit from His Father dwelling in him. After He was baptized by John, He was resurrected with the same body He had before He became a human being among us.

The body of the living saints is called the Temple of God because the spirit of God the Father dwells in them, and the living saints are Holy, as written earlier in 1 Corinthians 3:6-7. There are two types of resurrections, with two types of resurrected bodies, as I will explain later in this book. Children are born in the image of their parents, and the Living Creator God created humans to be His children, to form a Godly Family from us humans. God the Father will be the Father of all. Jesus Christ tells us to call His Father, our Father in Heaven, to pray to Him and glorify Him, as told in Matthew 6:9. In this manner, therefore, pray: Our Father in heaven, hallowed be Your name. Matthew 6:10 Your kingdom come. Your will be done on earth as it is in heaven.

The living saints call Father, their God the Father in Heaven, because the spirit of the Father dwells in them, as written earlier. The spirit from God the Father, in the living saints, makes the saints, begotten sons and daughters of God, as written in Hebrews 1:5. For to which of the angels did He ever say: "YOU ARE MY SON, TODAY I HAVE BEGOTTEN YOU?" And again: "I WILL BE TO HIM A FATHER, AND HE SHALL BE TO ME A SON"?

The spirit of God the Father dwelt in Jesus Christ, as written in John 17:21, that they all may be one, as You, Father, are in Me, and I in You; that they also may be one in Us, that the world may believe that You sent Me. John 17:22 And the glory which You gave Me I have given them, that they may be one just as We are one: John 17:23 I in them, and You in Me; that they may be made perfect in one, and that the world may know that You have sent Me, and have loved them as You have loved Me. John 17:24 "Father, I desire that they also whom You gave Me may be with Me where I am, that they may behold My glory which You have given Me; for You loved Me before the foundation of the world."

"ONE IN ALL," the spirit of God the Father binds all as one together with Jesus Christ. This makes the living saints, brothers and sisters of Jesus Christ. We are told to ask our Father in Heaven to send His Kingdom - Government to this earth, and to make this earth the same as it is in Heaven. The Apostle Paul wrote that the saints are the children of God, because they received the Spirit from God the Father, as written in Romans 8:16. The Spirit Himself bears witness with our spirit that we humans are children of God.

CAIN KILLED ANOTHER MAN NAMED ABEL

Many years HAD passed from when Adam and Eve were created, and the human population started to increase rapidly, throughout the entire world, when one man named Cain killed another man named Abel, as written in Genesis 4:8 Now Cain talked with Abel his brother; and it came to pass, when they were in the field, that Cain rose up against Abel his brother and killed him. This happened many years after Adam and Eve were created.

This man, Abel, was the first human being to die. He was the first witness to the results of eating the poisonous fruit, from Satan's forbidden tree, which Adam and Eve ate. This tree of death also brings sorrows. Until now, Adam and Eve did not know what death looked like, and the sorrow that brings with it, and how one feels, when a relative dies, but now when they saw the dead body of Abel, the taste of the fruit, which they ate from Satan's tree, came back to them, as bitter taste in their mouths, and realized their mistakes. But now, it was too late.

Now, when they witnessed the death of Abel, Adam and Eve knew that their lives were only of a limited time, as they were warned by their Living Creator God. Adam and Eve were deceived by Satan, and Satan had a win over the Living Creator God's creation, and over God's plan to create children, to form a Family. Satan knows the plan of the Living Creator God, and Satan wants to destroy the Creator's plan. Now the Creator God Himself had to become the second human Adam, born by a human woman, and confront Satan, as a human, so as not to let Satan win and destroy the Creator's plan. The Creator was born with a human body, when the Living Creator God became Jesus Christ.

Jesus Christ had to come as a human and allow Satan to butcher Him. Jesus Christ had to not yield to Satan, like the first Adam had done, even unto death, to be able to open up the door of the resurrection from the dead, for all humans, who die from the poisonous fruit that Satan fed to Adam and Eve. That poison runs through the bloodline of every human being, as formed in every human's DNA of chromosomes. As written earlier, Jesus Christ is the DOOR to Eternal Life by resurrection.

Jesus Christ was the second Adam as written in 1Corinthians 15:45. And so it is written, 'THE FIRST MAN ADAM BECAME A LIVING BEING." The last Adam became a life-giving spirit. Jesus Christ is the door to Eternal Life. Because of the interference of Satan, taking over our natural bodies, it became necessary to have two stages of life, having two different bodies, our natural body, and then a spiritual body, in the plan of the Living Creator God, to become the children of God, and to receive eternal life in God's Family forever, as it is written in 1

Corinthians 15:46 However, the spiritual is not first, but the natural, and afterward the spiritual.

We humans as a soul, are locked up into a physical, natural, mortal body; we still need to be changed, and to become encapsulated into an immortal, eternal, uncorrupted spiritual body, as written in 1 Corinthians 15:53 For this corruptible must put on incorruption, and this mortal must put on immortality. WE are mortal beings, and we need to become immortal by having an ETERNAL LIFE.

1 Corinthians 15:54 So when this corruptible has put on incorruption, and this mortal has put on immortality, then shall be brought to pass the saying that is written: "DEATH IS SWALLOWED UP IN VICTORY." And this is the VICTORY over Satan, who gives death. And at the end of it all, the Living Creator God will have a total win over Satan, and God will destroy Satan, never to exist anymore, as I will write later in this book. The first Adam was created from the dust of the earth; the second Adam, Jesus Christ, came down from Heaven, as written in 1 Corinthians 15:47.The first man was of the earth, made of dust; the second Man is the Lord from heaven. Genesis 2:7 And the LORD God formed man of the dust of the ground, and breathed into his nostrils the breath of life; and man became a living being.

When Jesus Christ's blood was discovered and tested, by Ron Wyatt, it was found that Jesus Christ's blood only had 24 X Chromosomes with only 1 Y chromosome in it, the Y chromosome was from His Father in Heaven, and 23 X Chromosomes were from his mother, while all humans have 46 Chromosomes, consisting of 23 Y Chromosomes from the father, and 23 X Chromosomes from the mother. Jesus Christ's blood did not have the poisons from the tree of Satan, which Adam had and passed on to every male. I will write more on this a little later.

Jesus Christ, was resurrected from the dead, as He surely did, with a Spirit uncorrupted body, by the spirit from His Father, that dwelt in Him when He was alive, at the time of His baptism, to open the door way for us humans, to be available for the saints, to resurrect from the dead by His same resurrection, resurrected with a spirit body.

And this is what happened: Satan confronted Jesus Christ face to face, in the same way as Satan did with Eve in the Garden of Eden. Jesus Christ confronted Satan, armed with the Spirit of His Father within Him, which He received when He was baptized, as written in Matthew 4:1.Then Jesus was led up by the Spirit into the wilderness to be tempted by the devil.

Matthew 4:2 And when He had fasted forty days and forty nights, afterward He was hungry. Matthew 4:3 Now when the tempter came to Him, he said, "If You are the Son of God, command that these stones become bread." Matthew 4:4 But He answered and said, "It is written, 'MAN SHALL NOT LIVE BY BREAD ALONE, BUT BY EVERY WORD THAT PROCEEDS FROM THE MOUTH OF GOD.'" Matthew 4:5 Then the devil took Him up into the holy city, set Him on the pinnacle of the temple.

Here, Jesus Christ is saying that we need to live by the words THAT PROCEED FROM THE MOUTH OF GOD. Do you recognize this? Keep away from those who don't teach you the words THAT PROCEED FROM THE MOUTH OF GOD, and they teach you traditions, customs and practices.

And here in this book, I am quoting to you words that proceeded from the mouth of God, which gives life. Matthew 4:6 and said to Him, "If You are the Son of God, throw Yourself down. For it is written: 'HE SHALL GIVE HIS ANGELS CHARGE OVER YOU,' and, IN THEIR HANDS THEY SHALL BEAR YOU UP, LEST YOU DASH YOUR FOOT AGAINST A STONE.'" Matthew 4:7 Jesus said to him, 'It is written again, 'YOU SHALL NOT TEMPT THE LORD YOUR GOD.'"

Matthew 4:8 Again, the devil took Him up on an exceedingly high mountain, and showed Him all the kingdoms of the world and their glory. Matthew 4:9 And he said to Him, "All these things I will give You if You will fall down and worship me."

All this planet is ruled and controlled by Satan. At present Satan owns everything. All the kingdoms and all the Governments of the world are ruled and controlled by Satan. At present, we are living under the kingdom of Satan. No matter where you are on this planet, you are a citizen of Satan, whether you know it or not.

Satan stole all this from Adam and Eve. If Satan did not have anything to offer, Jesus Christ would have said so. Matthew 4:10 Then Jesus said to him, "Away with you, Satan! For it is written, 'YOU SHALL WORSHIP THE LORD YOUR GOD, AND HIM ONLY YOU SHALL SERVE.'" Here, Jesus Christ is saying that we are to only worship the Living Creator God, and nobody, and no one else. In other words, Jesus Christ is saying that it is wrong to bow down and worship anything or anyone else, except the True Living Creator God.

The True Living Creator God wrote the Ten Commandments with His finger, Exodus 20:3 "You shall have no other gods before Me."

Exodus 20:4 "You shall not make for yourself a carved image—any likeness of anything that is in heaven above, or that is in the earth beneath, or that is in the water under the earth."

Exodus 20:5 You shall not bow down to them nor serve them. For I, the LORD your God, am a jealous God, visiting the iniquity of the fathers upon the children to the third and fourth generations of those who hate Me.

Exodus 20:6 But showing mercy to thousands, to those who love Me and keep My commandments. He says that He is a jealous God, as written in Exodus 20:5: "You shall not bow down to them nor serve them." For I, the LORD your God, am a jealous God. Matthew 4:11 Then the devil left Him, and behold, angels came and ministered to Him. Cain was cursed for killing Abel, as written in Genesis 4:11, So now you are cursed from the earth, which has opened its mouth to receive your brother's blood from your hand. Genesis 4:12 "When you till the ground, it shall no longer yield its strength to you. A fugitive and a vagabond, you shall be on the earth."

Cain was afraid that the rest of the people of that time, would turn on him, and will kill him, as written in Genesis 4:14 I shall be a fugitive and a vagabond on the earth, and it will happen that anyone who finds me will kill me." The Living Creator God did not want any harm to be done to Cain, or for Cain to be killed, as written in Genesis 4:15. And the LORD said to him, "Therefore, whoever kills Cain, vengeance shall be taken on him sevenfold." And the LORD set a mark on Cain, lest anyone finding him should kill him. Cain had to stand out from the rest of the people, for the people to recognize him and not to do him any harm, as they were commanded by the Living Creator God.

Cain had to carry his mark with him at all times, wherever he went, not to get killed, and the mark which God put on Cain had to be a permanent mark, and it had to become a part of his body, a visible mark that he could never remove it at any time. The word for Mark, in the original Text, is written אוֹת, meaning sign in appearance - Marked out from the rest. In other words, to appear different from the rest of humanity, that were made white. And to make Cain stand out from the rest, the Living Creator God changed Cain's skin from white to black, as I will provide proof

64

later in this article. Wherever Cain went, he stood out among the rest of the white people, and the people would remember that if they killed Cain, there would be a sevenfold vengeance on them. A descendant of Cain by the name of Lamech, who lived at the time of the floods of Noah, who had two wives, said the following, "If Cain shall be avenged sevenfold, Then Lamech seventy-sevenfold." I will write about him shortly.

Here is an example of how one black sheep stands out from the white ones. This is how Cain stood out from among the rest of humanity. The Living Creator God changed Cain's skin from white to black for two reasons: one was that the Living Creator God did not want Cain to be killed. The Living Creator God wanted Cain to be stood out from the rest of the white people, that when people see Cain will remember when The Living Creator God told them not to kill Cain.

My understanding is that an appropriate, permanent, visible mark was put on Cain so that Cain would not be able to refuse or remove it from himself. It had to be the change of the colour of his skin, of which he would not have control of, OR TO TAMPER WITH. God changed the colour of Cain's skin, from white to black, because God wanted Cain to live, and not to be killed. It was a sign that whenever the rest of humanity sees Black Cain, they remember that the Living Creator God had warned them not to harm Cain.

Anyone seeing black Cain had to remember God's warning, as written in Genesis 4:15 "And the LORD said to him, 'Therefore, whoever kills Cain, vengeance shall be taken on him sevenfold.'" Cain had children, and they would have been born black, on the same image as their father Cain. And now I will give the names of the descendants that carried Cain's genealogy to the last man, at Noah's Flood, and how God wanted Cain's bloodline to continue on, even after the flood, until this very day. The Living Creator God wants the black people to be called His children in His Family, like the rest of mankind. Romans 2:11 For there is no partiality with God.

Following is a list of the descendants of Cain.

Cain had a son named Enoch, as written in Genesis 4:17. And Cain knew his wife, and she conceived and bore Enoch. And he built a city, and called the name of the city after the name of his son, Enoch.

Genesis 4:18 To Enoch was born Irad; and Irad begot Mehujael, and Mehujael begot Methushael, and Methushael begot Lamech.

Genesis 4:19 Then Lamech took for himself two wives: the name of one was Adah, and the name of the second was Zillah.

Genesis 4:20 And Adah bore Jabal. He was the father of those who dwell in tents and have livestock.

Genesis 4:21 His brother's name was Jubal. He was the father of all those who play the harp and flute.

Genesis 4:22 And as for Zillah, she also bore Tubal-Cain, an instructor of every craftsman in bronze and iron. And the sister of Tubal-Cain was Naamah.

Genesis 4:23 Then Lamech said to his wives: "Adah and Zillah, hear my voice; Wives of Lamech, listen to my speech! For I have killed a man for wounding me, even a young man for hurting me.

Genesis 4:24 "If Cain shall be avenged sevenfold, Then Lamech seventy-sevenfold."

This Lamech was a black man from the lineage of black Cain. He lived at the same time as Noah. Please remember this, because another man by the same name of Lamech, from the lineage of Adam, from a different genealogy, appears at the same time, of the great flood.

Cain was wicked and belonged to Satan, as written in 1 John 3:11. For this is the message that you heard from the beginning, that we should love one another.

1 John 3:12 not as Cain, who was of the wicked one and murdered his brother. And why did he murder him? Because his works were evil and his brothers were righteous. From this verse, we learn that Abel was a righteous man.

Now we begin a different genealogy, distinct from the one I just provided for Cain.

Genesis 5:1 This is the book of the genealogy of Adam. On the day that God created man, He made him in the likeness of God.

Genesis 5:2 He created them male and female, and blessed them and called them Mankind, in the day they were created.

Genesis 5:3 And Adam lived one hundred and thirty years, and begot a son in his own likeness, after his image, and named him Seth.

Genesis 5:4 After he begot Seth, the days of Adam were eight hundred years; and he had sons and daughters.

Genesis 5:5 So all the days that Adam lived were nine hundred and thirty years; and he died.

I like to insert the following regarding the death of Adam. Adam and Eve were told that if they ate the fruit from the tree of Satan, they would die on the same day. Did their Living Creator God tell them a lie, did He lied to them, when they did not die on the same day when they ate Satan's deadly fruit? as written in Genesis 2:16 And the LORD God commanded the man, saying, "Of every tree of the garden you may freely eat; Genesis 2:17 but of the tree of the knowledge of good and evil you shall not eat, for in the day that you eat of it you shall surely die." Satan convinced Eve that their Living Creator God was a liar, as written in Genesis 3:4. Then the serpent said to the woman, "You will not surely die." When Adam and Eve woke up, the day after eating Satan's fruit, they were convinced that Satan told them the truth, about their Living Creator God being a liar, because they woke up from their sleep the next morning, and found themselves still alive.

Sure enough, they did not die on that same very day, when they ate from Satan's fruit, which brought death to all mankind. The Living Creator God did not create us humans to kill us, but Satan brought in death on us all. The point I would like to bring out is, that Adam died within the one thousand years, when he was nine hundred and thirty years old, within one thousand years, and one thousand years to the Living Creator God, is as one day, as written in 2 Peter 3:8 But, beloved, do not forget this one thing, that with the Lord one day is as a thousand years, and a thousand years as one day.

69

This makes it clear what the Living Creator God meant when He told them that they would die on the same day they ate the fruit from Satan. The same day, Adam and Eve were told that they would die, but not within one thousand years. There is no record of any human who lived for over a thousand years, so far. We may see some humans living for over a thousand years. Later on, when Jesus Christ returns, He will be ruling this planet, with Satan in prison, and death will be in prison with him. I will write about this shortly.

Genesis 5:6 Seth lived one hundred and five years, and begot Enosh.

Genesis 5:7 After he begot Enosh, Seth lived eight hundred and seven years, and had sons and daughters.

Genesis 5:8 So all the days of Seth were nine hundred and twelve years; and he died.

Genesis 5:9 Enosh lived ninety years, and begot Cainan.

Genesis 5:10 After he begot Cainan, Enosh lived eight hundred and fifteen years, and had sons and daughters.

Genesis 5:11 So all the days of Enosh were nine hundred and five years; and he died.

Genesis 5:12 Cainan lived seventy years, and begot Mahalalel.

Genesis 5:13 After he begot Mahalalel, Cainan lived eight hundred and forty years, and had sons and daughters.

Genesis 5:14 So all the days of Cainan were nine hundred and ten years; and he died.

Genesis 5:15 Mahalalel lived sixty-five years, and begot Jared.

Genesis 5:16 After he begot Jared, Mahalalel lived eight hundred and thirty years, and had sons and daughters.

Genesis 5:17 So all the days of Mahalalel were eight hundred and ninety-five years; and he died.

Genesis 5:18 Jared lived one hundred and sixty-two years, and begot Enoch.

Genesis 5:19 After he begot Enoch, Jared lived eight hundred years, and had sons and daughters.

Genesis 5:20 So all the days of Jared were nine hundred and sixty-two years; and he died.

Genesis 5:21 Enoch lived sixty-five years and begot Methuselah.

Genesis 5:22 After he begot Methuselah, Enoch walked with God three hundred years, and had sons and daughters.

Genesis 5:23 So all the days of Enoch were three hundred and sixty-five years.

Genesis 5:24 And Enoch walked with God; and he was not, for God took him.

Genesis 5:25 Methuselah lived one hundred and eighty-seven years, and begot Lamech.

Genesis 5:26 After he begot Lamech, Methuselah lived seven hundred and eighty-two years, and had sons and daughters.

Genesis 5:27 So all the days of Methuselah were nine hundred and sixty-nine years; and he died.

Genesis 5:28 Lamech lived one hundred and eighty-two years, and had a son.

Genesis 5:29 And he called his name Noah, saying, "This one will comfort us concerning our work and the toil of our hands, because of the ground which the LORD has cursed."

Now we see, that at the time of Noah, we have two men with the same name of Lamech, living at the same time, from two different genealogies. One Lamech is a black man, from the genealogy of Cain, and the other Lamech is a white man from the direct genealogy of Adam. As written earlier, Noah was the son of white Lamech. At this time, these two genealogies are merging into one, as the two men named Lamech are merging through marriage, with Noah marrying a black wife, from the bloodline of Cain, as I will provide proof of shortly.

The Living Creator God prepared all this from the very beginning to preserve a heritage of the black race people during Noah's flood. This shows how much the Living Creator God cares for black people, not to let them become extinct. Isaiah 46:9 Remember the former things of old, For I am God, and there is no other; I am God, and there is none like Me, Isaiah 46:10 Declaring the end from the beginning, And from ancient times things that are not yet done, Saying, 'My counsel shall stand, And I will do all My pleasure,'

The Living Creator God prepared everything from the beginning, even before His Creation. The Apostle Peter confirms this, that Jesus Christ was in the plan of the Living Creator God, to be offered like a lamb, from before the foundations of this earth. And this earth is many billions of years old. It was in the Living Creator God's plan that if the first Adam failed, the Living Creator God Himself would come and be the second Adam, as I have already mentioned earlier. Later on in this article, I will show you something, of how The Living Creator God created and prepared, during His creation of this planet earth, billions of years ago, to be a sign, for us living at this time now, to show us that the return of Jesus Christ is imminent, ready to take place. And that was the creation of the Azure Window in West Gozo, Malta.

At that time of Noah, the earth's Population became so wicked, that the Living Creator God was sorry that He had created Adam, and Eve, and was contemplating to destroy all and everything, what He had created and made, as written in Genesis 6:5 Then the LORD saw that the wickedness of man was great in the earth, and that every intent of the thoughts of his heart was only evil continually.

Genesis 6:6 And the LORD was sorry that He had made man on the earth, and He was grieved in His heart. Genesis 6:7 So the LORD said, "I will destroy man whom I have created from the face of the earth, both man and beast, creeping thing and birds of the air, for I am sorry that I have made them." The Living Creator God decided to destroy everything. Genesis 6:8 But Noah found grace in the eyes of the LORD.

The present Earth's Population has become wicked to the same proportion as it was in the days of Noah. This time, the destruction will not be by a water flood, because the Living Creator God made the following covenant with Noah, as written in Genesis 9:11 Thus I establish My covenant with you: Never again shall all flesh be cut off by the waters of the flood; never again shall there be a flood to destroy the earth." Genesis 9:12 And God said: "This is the sign of the covenant which I make between Me and you, and every living creature that is with you, for perpetual generations: Genesis 9:13 I set My rainbow in the cloud, and it shall be for the sign of the covenant between Me and the earth.

This time, fire will be used. Isaiah 1:7 Your country is desolate, your cities are burned with fire; Strangers devour your land in your presence, And it is desolate, as overthrown by strangers. Isaiah 29:6 You will be punished by the LORD of hosts with thunder and earthquake and great noise, with storm and tempest and the flame of devouring fire. Isaiah 47:14 Behold, they shall be as stubble. The fire shall burn them; They shall not deliver themselves from the power of the flame. It shall not be a coal to be warmed by, nor a fire to sit before! Zephaniah 1:18 Neither their silver nor their gold shall be able to deliver them in the day of the LORD's wrath; But the whole land shall be devoured by the fire of His jealousy, for He will make speedy riddance of all those who dwell in the land. Revelation 9:17 And thus I saw the horses in the vision: those who sat on them had breastplates of fiery red, hyacinth blue, and sulfur yellow; and the heads of the horses were like the heads of lions; and out of their mouths came fire, smoke, and brimstone.

Revelation 9:18 By these three plagues, a third of mankind was killed—by the fire and the smoke and the brimstone which came out of their mouths. FIRE COMING DOWN FROM THE SKY is going to be used to wipe out part of this present wicked Population. The end result will be leaving only 10% alive from the present total of the entire world population. Revelation 13:13 He performs great signs, so that he even makes fire come down from heaven on the earth in the sight of men. Could this be nuclear missiles raining from the sky?

Here we read that only one man, whose name was Noah, was the only righteous man among the billions of people of that time. For the sake of one single man, the Living Creator God decided to save this single man and his family, and repented from destroying the whole creation. There were billions of people destroyed by the flood, which God sent on the planet Earth. Here we only find written Noah's name, and his family is not mentioned. But for the sake of Noah's righteousness, the Living Creator God also saved Noah's family.

God told Noah what He had decided to do, as written in Genesis 6:17. And behold, I Myself am bringing floodwaters on the earth, to destroy from under heaven all flesh, in which is the breath of life; everything that is on the earth shall die.

Genesis 6:18 But I will establish My covenant with you; and you shall go into the ark—you, your sons, your wife, and your sons' wives with you.

Genesis 7:4 For after seven more days I will cause it to rain on the earth forty days and forty nights, and I will destroy from the face of the earth all living things that I have made." Genesis 7:12 And the rain was on the earth forty days and forty nights.

Genesis 8:15 Then God spoke to Noah, saying,

Genesis 8:16 "Go out of the ark, you and your wife, and your sons and your sons' wives with you.

Gen 8:18 So Noah went out, and his sons and his wife and his sons' wives with him.

Noah's Ark has been found in Turkey. And here are photos of it.

I will show the inscription, inscribed and engraved on a stone billboard, by Noah, that was found near where the ark was found in Turkey, with the images inscribed in stone portraying the eight people who were in the ark, who survived the great flood. Many other inscriptions were found on the stones, built as a billboard, where the ark landed.

This is the Stone Billboard, with many inscriptions engraved by Noah, following, I will insert the portrait inscription showing us the real features of the eight people that came out of the ark. This is a very clear picture of who is who.

This photo is from the portrait that Noah inscribed and engraved on the stone Billboard.

On the left is Noah and his wife. His wife was a black woman, and she is depicted as black on the billboard. According to biblical genealogy, Noah's wife was a descendant of Cain, the son of Adam. The Living Creator God put a permanent MARK on Cain, after Cain killed Abel, so that wherever he is seen, he is not to kill him, as written earlier in this article. On the stone billboard were many other inscriptions, engraved in great detail.

In this inscription, engraved on the stone billboard, we find, on the left, Noah. Next to Noah is his black wife.

Next to his mother, in the front row, is Shem; in the middle of the three sons is Ham, and then Japheth. And behind the three sons are their three wives. The first wife from the left is Shem's wife. The middle wife is Ham's wife. The one on the far right is Japheth's wife - Japheth and his wife have yellow skin.

This is a significant discovery, as the inscription, engraved on the stone billboard, was found alongside many other inscriptions, providing us with valuable information. This inscription on the discovered stone billboard confirms that Noah's wife was a black woman, a descendant of black Cain. It also confirms that one of the three sons of Noah, by the name of Ham, was also a black man. And when we study the following chart of Ham's generations and the locations of his dark-skinned descendants around the world, we gain a very clear picture of the past. All those with a dark skin shade have some connection to Ham.

When we study the behavior of the sons of Ham, as recorded in the Bible, we come to a conclusion about the present generation and how they are behaving among us, all around the world.

In the following chart, we have a record of four of Ham's sons. Study this chart thoroughly, as it is essential to know who is who and where they reside in the present-day locations around the world.

We are going to experience wars in the near future. Billions of people are going to die, and by having this information as I am writing here, you will have an advantage over many others, to know who is fighting whom.

As of this writing, we are witnessing a war in the Gaza Strip. From the following chart, we know that the Philistines descended from Mizraim, who was the son of Ham. They are part of the dark colour people. All dark colour people are related to Ham, the son of Noah. The majority of black people are found in Africa.

19 NOVEMBER 2024

List Of African Countries By Population

Nigeria. (2024 est.) 228,181,000.

Democratic Republic of the Congo. (2024 est.) 115,403,000.

Ethiopia. (2024 est.) 109,900,000.

Égypte (2024 est.) 106647000.

Tanzania. (2024 est.) 65,444,000.

South Africa. (2024 est.) 64,701,000.

Kenya. (2024 est.) 51,563,000.

Sudan. (2024 est.) 47,653,000.

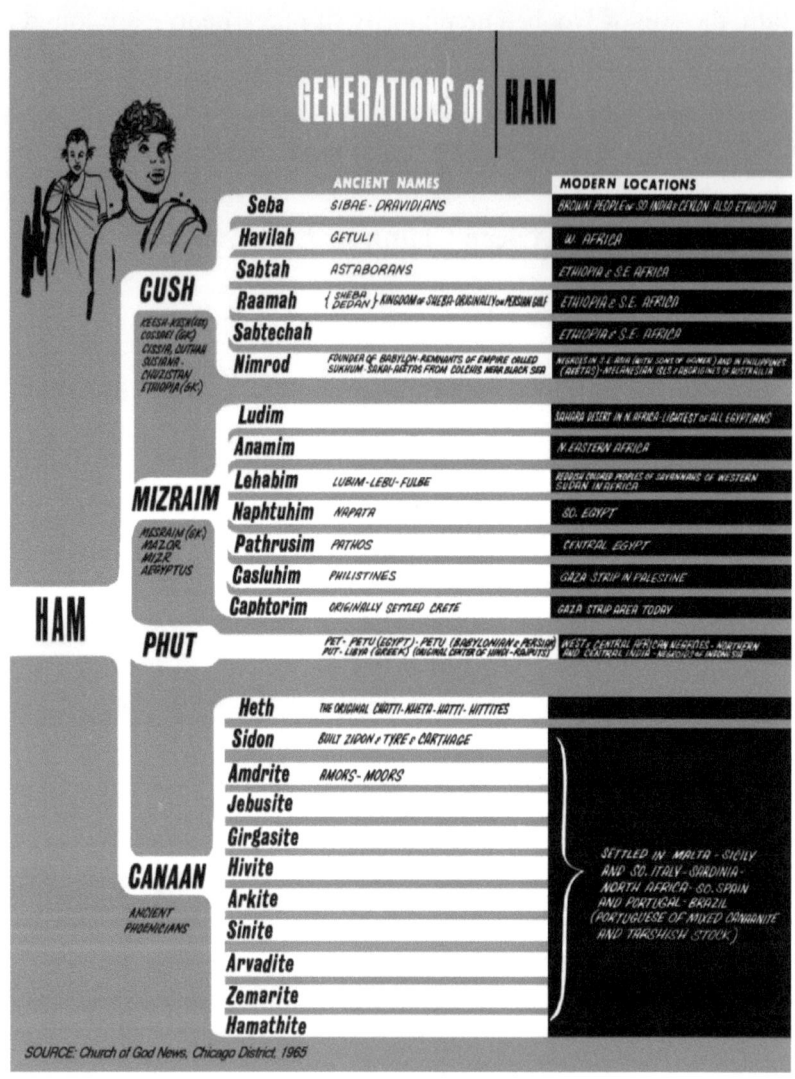

GENERATIONS of HAM

	ANCIENT NAMES	MODERN LOCATIONS
CUSH KUESH-ASSYRIAN) COLCHOS (GK) CUSSIA, OUTHAH SUSIANA - CHRISTIAN ETHIOPIA (GK.)		
Seba	SIBAE - DRAVIDIANS	BROWN PEOPLE or SO INDIA & CEYLON ALSO ETHIOPIA
Havilah	GETULI	W. AFRICA
Sabtah	ASTABORANS	ETHIOPIA & S.E. AFRICA
Raamah	{ SHEBA DEDAN } KINGDOM of SHEBA-ORIGINALLY on PERSIAN GULF	ETHIOPIA & S.E. AFRICA
Sabtechah		ETHIOPIA & S.E. AFRICA
Nimrod	FOUNDER OF BABYLON-REMNANTS OF EMPIRE CALLED SUKHUM - SAKAI-AKHTAS FROM COLCHIS NEAR BLACK SEA	NEGROES IN S.E. ASIA (WITH SONS OF GOMER) AND IN PHILIPPINES (AAETAS)-MELANESIAN (&S ABORIGINES OF AUSTRALIA
MIZRAIM MIZRAIM (GK.) AMZOR MIZR AEGYPTUS		
Ludim		SAHARA DESERT IN N. AFRICA-LIGHTEST OF ALL EGYPTIANS
Anamim		N. EASTERN AFRICA
Lehabim	LUBIM-LEBU-FULBE	REDDISH COLORED PEOPLES OF SAVANNAHS OF WESTERN SUDAN IN AFRICA
Naphtuhim	NAPATA	SO. EGYPT
Pathrusim	PATHOS	CENTRAL EGYPT
Casluhim	PHILISTINES	GAZA STRIP IN PALESTINE
Caphtorim	ORIGINALLY SETTLED CRETE	GAZA STRIP AREA TODAY
PHUT	PET - PETU (EGYPT) - PETU (BABYLONIAN & PERSIA) PUT - LIBYA (GREEK) (ORIGINAL CENTER OF LIBYA-RAJPUTS)	(WEST & CENTRAL AFR) OR NEGROES - NORTHERN AND CENTRAL INDIA - NEGROES? or INDONESIA
CANAAN ANCIENT PHOENICIANS		
Heth	THE ORIGINAL CHATTI-KHETA-HATTI-HITTITES	
Sidon	BUILT ZIDON & TYRE & CARTHAGE	
Amdrite	AMORS - MOORS	
Jebusite		
Girgasite		SETTLED IN MALTA - SICILY AND SO. ITALY - SARDINIA - NORTH AFRICA- SO. SPAIN AND PORTUGAL - BRAZIL (PORTUGUESE OF MIXED CANAANITE AND TARSHISH STOCK)
Hivite		
Arkite		
Sinite		
Arvadite		
Zemarite		
Hamathite		

SOURCE: Church of God News, Chicago District, 1965

These are the modern-day nations from the lineage of Cain, through Noah's black son Ham.

Genesis 9:18 Now the sons of Noah who went out of the ark were Shem, Ham, and Japheth. And Ham was the father of Canaan.

Genesis 9:19 These three were the sons of Noah, and from these, the whole earth was populated.

Ham did an evil deed to his father. Ham fathered an illegitimate son, when he slept with his own mother, the black wife of his father, Noah. Ham had intercourse with his mother, Noah's wife, and his mother got pregnant by her son Ham, and she bore a son. Ham named his illegitimate son Canaan, as written earlier and is recorded in Genesis 9:18. When Ham had intercourse with his mother, Ham bragged to his two brothers, Shem and Japheth, that he had slept with his mother, and that he had intercourse with her, as written in Genesis 9:22. And Ham, the father of Canaan, saw the nakedness of his father and told his two brothers outside, after he had intercourse with his mother. Ham, by having intercourse with his mother, the scripture tells us that he uncovered his father's nakedness, as written in Leviticus 18:8 The nakedness of your father's wife you shall not uncover; it is your father's nakedness.

This verse forbids a son to uncover his mother from her clothes, and to have intercourse with his mother, because by doing this act, the son uncovers his father's nakedness. And this is exactly what Ham did; he discovered his father's nakedness.

When Noah learned and discovered what his son Ham had done with his mother, when Noah's wife gave birth to Canaan, Noah cursed the illegitimate son of Ham, whose name was Canaan. After Canaan was born, as written in Genesis 9:25, he said, "Cursed be Canaan; A servant of servants He shall be to his brethren."

Now that you have learned about the origins of the black people and their current locations, I will show you how the world's populations have descended from Noah's other two sons, Shem and Japheth.

Study the following pictures carefully, and you will learn a lot about different people around the world.

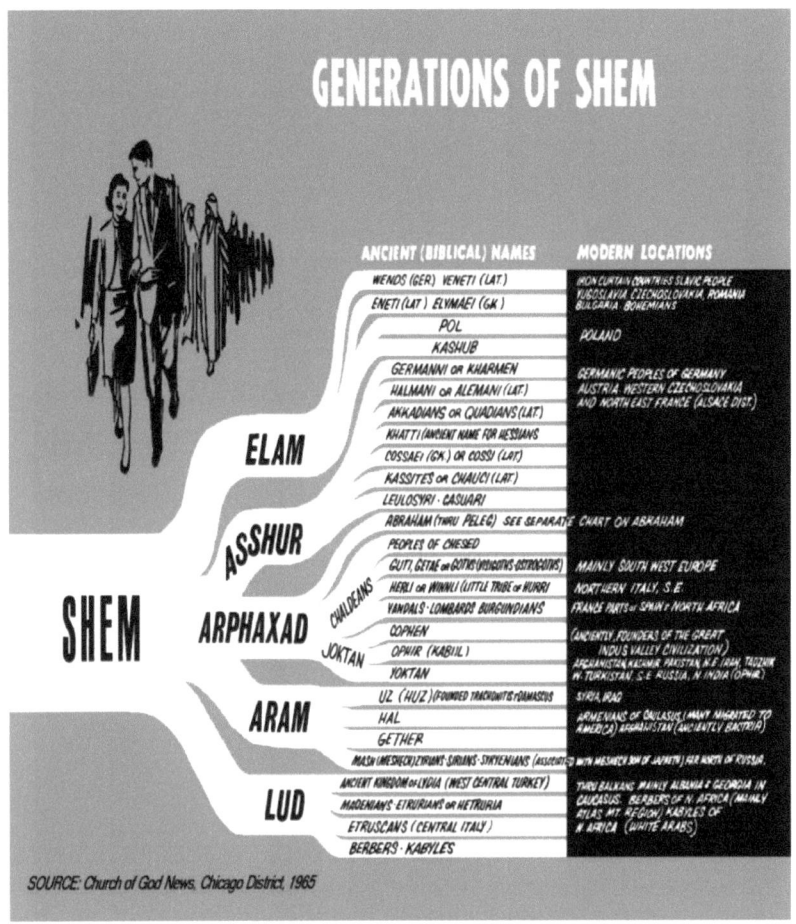

GENERATIONS OF SHEM

ANCIENT (BIBLICAL) NAMES	MODERN LOCATIONS
WENDS (GER.) VENETI (LAT.)	IRON CURTAIN COUNTRIES SLAVIC PEOPLE
ENETI (LAT.) ELYMAEI (GK.)	YUGOSLAVIA CZECHOSLOVAKIA, ROMANIA BULGARIA, BOHEMIANS
POL	POLAND
KASHUB	
GERMANNI OR KHARMEN	GERMANIC PEOPLES OF GERMANY
HALMANI OR ALEMANI (LAT.)	AUSTRIA, WESTERN CZECHOSLOVAKIA AND NORTH EAST FRANCE (ALSACE DIST.)
AKKADIANS OR QUADIANS (LAT.)	
KHATTI (ANCIENT NAME FOR HESSIANS)	
COSSAEI (GK.) OR COSSI (LAT.)	
KASSITES OR CHAUCI (LAT.)	
LEULOSYRI · CASUARI	
ABRAHAM (THRU PELEG) SEE SEPARATE CHART ON ABRAHAM	
PEOPLES OF CHESED	
GUTI, GETAE OR GOTHS (VISIGOTHS-OSTROGOTHS)	MAINLY SOUTH WEST EUROPE
HERLI OR WINNLI (LITTLE TRIBE OR HURRI)	NORTHERN ITALY, S.E.
VANDALS · LOMBARDS BURGUNDIANS	FRANCE PARTS OF SPAIN & NORTH AFRICA
COPHEN	(ANCIENTLY FOUNDERS OF THE GREAT INDUS VALLEY CIVILIZATION)
OPHIR (KABUL)	AFGHANISTAN KASHMIR PAKISTAN, N.E. IRAN, TADZHIK W. TURKISTAN, S.E. RUSSIA, N. INDIA (OPHIR)
YOKTAN	
UZ (HUZ) (FOUNDED TRACHONITIS & DAMASCUS)	SYRIA, IRAQ
HAL	ARMENIANS OF CAUCASUS (MANY MIGRATED TO AMERICA) AFGHANISTAN (ANCIENTLY BACTRIA)
GETHER	
MASH (MESHECK)(TYRUS) SIRIANS · SYRYENIANS (ASSOCIATES WITH MESHECK SON OF JAPHETH) FAR NORTH OF RUSSIA	
ANCIENT KINGDOM OR LYDIA (WEST CENTRAL TURKEY)	THRU BALKANS MAINLY ALBANIA & GEORGIA IN
MADENIANS ETRURIANS OR HETRURIA	CAUCASUS. BERBERS OF N. AFRICA (MAINLY ATLAS MT. REGION) KABYLES OF
ETRUSCANS (CENTRAL ITALY)	N AFRICA (WHITE ARABS)
BERBERS · KABYLES	

ELAM
ASSHUR
ARPHAXAD
CHALDEANS
JOKTAN
SHEM
ARAM
LUD

SOURCE: Church of God News, Chicago District, 1965

Here we have five sons mentioned from Shem. The most important son is Arphaxad, from whom Abraham comes.

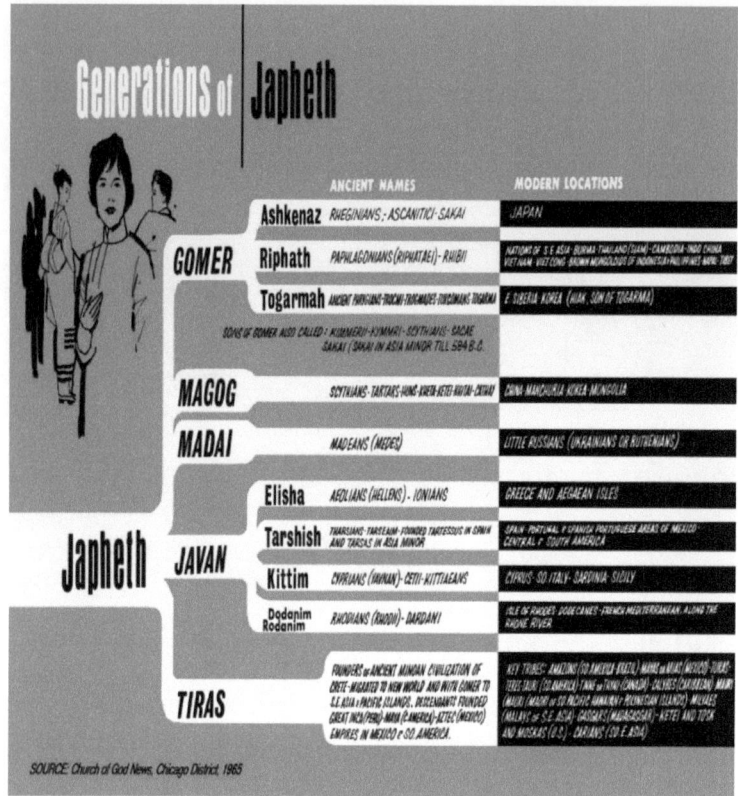

Generations of Japheth

		ANCIENT NAMES	MODERN LOCATIONS
	Ashkenaz	RHEGINIANS ; ASCANITICI-SAKAI	JAPAN
GOMER	Riphath	PAPHLAGONIANS (RIPHATAEI)- RHIBII	NATIONS OF S.E. ASIA-BURMA-THAILAND (SIAM) - CAMBODIA-INDO CHINA VIETNAM - VIET CONG -BROWN MONGOLOIDS OF INDONESIA-PHILIPPINES -WANG- THAI?
	Togarmah	ANCIENT PHRYGIANS-TROCMI-TURKMADES-TURCOMANS-TOGARMA	E.SIBERIA-KOREA (ASAN, SON OF TOGARMA)
	SONS OF GOMER ALSO CALLED : KUMMERII-KYMMRI- SCYTHIANS- SACAE SAKAI (SAKAI IN ASIA MINOR TILL 594 B.C.		
MAGOG		SCYTHIANS- TARTARS-HUNS-KHETA-KETEI-KATAI-CATHAI	CHINA-MANCHURIA-KOREA-MONGOLIA
MADAI		MADEANS (MEDES)	LITTLE RUSSIANS (UKRAINIANS OR RUTHENIANS)
	Elisha	AEOLIANS (HELLENS) - IONIANS	GREECE AND AEGAEAN ISLES
	Tarshish	THARSIANS- TARSEUM- FOUNDED TARTESSUS IN SPAIN AND TARSAS IN ASIA MINOR	SPAIN- PORTUGAL & SPANISH-PORTUGUESE AREAS OF MEXICO- CENTRAL & SOUTH AMERICA
JAVAN	Kittim	CYPRIANS (HAINAN)- CETII- KITTIAEANS	CYPRUS- SO. ITALY- SARDINIA- SICILY
	Dodanim Rodanim	RHODIANS (RHODII)- DARDANI	ISLE OF RHODES- DODECANES- FRENCH MEDITERRANEAN, ALONG THE RHONE RIVER
TIRAS		FOUNDERS OF ANCIENT MINOAN CIVILIZATION OF CRETE-MIGRATED TO NEW WORLD AND WITH GOMER TO S.E.ASIA & PACIFIC ISLANDS, DESCENDANTS FOUNDED GREAT INCA (PERU)-MAYA (C.AMERICA)-AZTEC (MEXICO) EMPIRES IN MEXICO & SO. AMERICA.	KEY TRIBES: AMAZONS (SO.AMERICA-BRAZIL) MAYAS or MAYAS (MEXICO)-TURAS- TERES-TAUK (SO.AMERICA) TANA or TAINO (CANADA) - CALVES (CARIBBEAN) MAM (MAUI) (MADAI or SO.PACIFIC-HAWAIIAN)- POLYNESIAN (ISLANDS) MEENEES (MALAYS of S.E.ASIA)-DASOARES (MADAGASCAR)- KETEI AND TOTSK AND MOSKAS (U.S.) - DARIANS (COD E.ASIA)

SOURCE: Church of God News, Chicago District, 1965

Here, we have recorded five additional sons from Japheth. As mentioned earlier, Japheth and his wife, as I understand from the inscription found on the stone billboard, are from whom the yellow-skinned people descended. And this chart says it all. Study this chart to fully understand what I am writing for you.

Generations of Abraham

	ANCIENT NAMES	MODERN LOCATIONS
ASHER	BELGAE	BELGIUM-LUXEMBOURG
REUBEN	NORMANS-FRANKS	FRANCE
SIMEON	SIMONS ANCIENTLY IN WALES & S. ENGLAND	SCATTERED (IN ENGLAND)
LEVI		SCATTERED (IN ENGLAND)
JUDAH (SEE NOTE BELOW)	MILESIAN KINGS IN IRELAND (ZEPHARDIN LINE) IBERIA-FIR BOLGS OF ZARA LINE	JEWS (SCATTERED WORLD WIDE)
ZEBULUN	FRISIANS- DACI- BELGAE	HOLLAND
ISSACHAR	EPITALITES- SKERA- SUOMES-FENN	FINLAND
DAN	TURTHA DE DANAANS- DANES- DANAI MILESIANS- NEMEDIANS - FIR BOLGS	DENMARK-IRELAND
GAD		SWITZERLAND
NAPHTALI	EPITALITES- SKERA - SUIONES-DACI	SWEDEN
BENJAMIN	NORSEMEN- NORTHMEN- VIKINGS SVEAR - SUIONES- DACI	NORWAY ICELAND
EPHRAIM	SCOTS-ANGLES-SAXONS- BRITONS NORMANS- JUTES	ENGLAND
MANASSEH	EAST ANGELS- SAXONS	UNITED STATES

JACOB

GENERAL NAMES OF JACOB'S DESCENDANTS:

JOSEPH

PARTHIANS- PHOENICIANS-SCYTHIANS- SCOLOTI- DAHA (DAHAE) CIMMERIANS- GIMIRI- KIMRI- GOTHS GETAE- DANAI- FENNI- EPITALITES (WHITE HUNS)- CELTS- GAULS- GALLI- IBERIANS

ISAAC — ESAU : TURKEY - OTTOMAN EMPIRE THRU TEMAN (ANCIENTLY THE FOMORIANS IN IRISH HISTORY)

THRU SARAH

EBER (ALL EBER'S DESCENDANTS ARE CALLED HEBREWS)

ABRAHAM

THRU KETURAH (AFTER SARAH DIED)

Asshurim : N. GERMANY (MANY IMMIGRATED TO U.S.) SHEBA- SINE- SWABIAN GERMANY

Medan-Median : WITH MADAI (MEDES) OF JAPHETH IN N. RUSSIA- PERSIANS (BUSINESSMEN OF IRAN) PARSEES IN INDIA-BRAHMANS OF INDIA (WEALTHIER CLASS) ANCIENTLY KINGDOM OF MITANNI

Letushim : LETTISH PEOPLE ON S.E. SHORES OF BALTIC SEA (FORMERLY ESTONIA-LATVIA LITHUANIA- N.W. RUSSIA (MANY OF THESE MIGRATED TO THE U.S.A.)

THRU HAGAR

ISHMAEL : ARABS OF ARABIA THROUGHOUT N. IRAQ- IRAN- N.W. INDIA- ACROSS N. AFRICA- ARABS

LOT (ABRAHAMS' NEPHEW) : MOAB- AMMON (JORDANIAN ARABS)

JUDAH (SEE ABOVE CHART) : PHAREZ LINE (INCLUDES DAVID) RULED IN PALESTINE LONG BEFORE CAPTIVITY ZARA LINE RULED IN IRELAND FROM SHORTLY AFTER EXODUS THE TWO LINES THRU HEREMON (ZARA LINE) AND TEA TEPHI (PHAREZ LINE) UNITED IN IRELAND 590 TO 569 B.C.

SOURCE: Church of God News, Chicago District, 1965

Here we have six sons of Abraham, from three wives.

Now study this chart of the sons of Jacob and where Jacob's descendants are today.

	ANCIENT NAMES	MODERN LOCATIONS
ASHER	BELGAE	BELGIUM·LUXEMBOURG
REUBEN	NORMANS·FRANKS	FRANCE
SIMEON	SIMONII-ANCIENTLY IN WALES & S. ENGLAND	SCATTERED (IN ENGLAND)
LEVI		SCATTERED (IN ENGLAND)
JUDAH (SEE NOTE BELOW)	MILESIAN KINGS of IRELAND (SEPHARDIM LINE) IBERII-FIR BOLGS of ZARA LINE	JEWS (SCATTERED WORLD WIDE)
ZEBULUN	FRISIANS·DACI·BELGAE	HOLLAND
ISSACHAR	EPHTALITES·SVEAR·SUIONES·FENNI	FINLAND
DAN	TUATHA DE DANAANS·DANES·DANAI MILESIANS·NEMEDIANS·FIR BOLGS	DENMARK·IRELAND
GAD		SWITZERLAND
NAPHTALI	EPHTALITES·SVEAR·SUIONES·DACI	SWEDEN
BENJAMIN	NORSEMEN·NORTHMEN·VIKINGS SVEAR·SUIONES·DACI	NORWAY ICELAND
JOSEPH — EPHRAIM	SCOTS·ANGELS·SAXONS·BRITONS NORMANS·JUTES	ENGLAND
JOSEPH — MANASSEH	EAST ANGELS·SAXONS	UNITED STATES

JACOB

GENERAL NAMES OF JACOB'S DESCENDANTS:

PARTHIANS·PHOENICIANS·SCYTHIANS·SCOLOTI·SAKRI (SACAE) CIMMERIANS·GIMIRI·KIMRI·GOTHS GETAE·DANAI·FENNI·EPHTALITES (WHITE HUNS)·CELTS·GAULS·GALLI·IBERIANS

Here we have mentioned twelve sons of Jacob, from four wives.

Matthew 5:8 Blessed are the pure in heart, for they shall see God.

Matthew 5:9Blessed are the peacemakers, for they shall be called sons of God.

Matthew 5:10 Blessed are those who are persecuted for righteousness' sake, for theirs is the kingdom of heaven.

The Kingdom of Heaven - God's Government on this earth, the one Jesus Christ tells us to ask our Father for, will be established on this earth in the next few years.

You may ask me how I know this. Luke 11:1 Now it came to pass, as He was praying in a certain place, when He ceased, that one of His disciples said to Him, "Lord, teach us to pray, as John also taught his disciples." Luke 11:2 So He said to them, "When you pray, say: Our Father in heaven, Hallowed be Your name. Your kingdom come. Your will be done on earth as it is in heaven.

Satan is in charge of all the present kingdoms on this planet. Satan is ruling this entire earth, and Satan showed and offered to give it all to Jesus Christ, as mentioned earlier, the entire world kingdoms and governments are all Satan's kingdoms, when he tempted Jesus Christ, as written in Matthew 4:8Again, the devil took Him up on an exceedingly high mountain, and showed Him all the kingdoms of the world and their glory.

Matthew 4:9 And he said to Him, "All these things I will give You if You will fall down and worship me."

If Satan did not have all the kingdoms of the world, Jesus Christ would have told Satan that he had nothing to offer Him.

Yes, Satan is the god who is ruling this planet. The Living Creator God's Kingdom is going to be established on this earth, in the near future, in the next few years, and you, reading this article, may still be alive to witness this. The present ruler of this world will be locked up for one thousand years, as I have explained many times in this book. 2Corinthians 4:4 whose minds the god of this age has blinded, who do not believe, lest the light of the gospel of the glory of Christ, who is the image of God, should shine on them. Revelation 20:2 He laid hold of the dragon, that serpent of old, who is the Devil and Satan, and bound him for a thousand years;

Believe it or not, Satan is the god of this world, and the whole world population is worshipping Satan, in one way or another, in some shape or form.

The Prophet Daniel prophesied the soon-coming Kingdom of the Living Creator God thousands of years ago. Daniel wrote that Satan's kingdoms will be destroyed, as stated in Daniel 2:43. As you saw iron mixed with ceramic clay, they will mingle with the seed of men, but they will not adhere to one another, just as iron does not mix with clay.

Daniel 2:44 And in the days of these kings the God of heaven will set up a kingdom which shall never be destroyed; and the kingdom shall not be left to other people; it shall break in pieces and consume all these kingdoms, and it shall stand forever.

Satan's ruling time in this world is nearly over. No matter what your belief is, or what type of life you are living, with your customs and traditions, you may be following and doing what Satan wants you to do. Your belief and what you are doing, your whole way of life, depend on the place you were born in. You would be a Muslim if you were born in an Arab region. You would be a Buddhist if you were born in Tibet. You would be a Hindu if you were born in India. You would be calling yourself a Christian if you were born in the Western world. This entire planet is ruled and is under Satan, the god of confusion, no matter which corner of the earth you live in or travel to.

First and foremost, we should recognize the times in which we live. We must consider the conditions and events happening all around us. It is written in Matthew 24:3 that the disciples asked Jesus Christ to give them the sign of his coming back: "Tell us, when will these things be? And what will be the sign of Your coming, and of the end of the age?"

Jesus Christ gave the signs that we should be looking for, as listed in Matthew 24. There are too many to write them all in here, in this short article.

Jesus Christ wants us to discern the times in which we live, to be aware of what is happening around us and around the world. Jesus Christ wants us to discern and be aware of the perilous times in which we are living right now. Jesus Christ, admonished the Pharisees and the Sadducees, for not discerning the times they were living in, as written in Matthew 16:3 and in the morning, 'It will be foul weather today, for the sky is red and threatening.' Hypocrites! You know how to discern the face of the sky, but you cannot discern the signs of the times.

Jesus Christ wants us to be on our guard, so that the day does not come upon us unaware, as written in Matthew 24:42: 'Watch therefore, for you do not know what hour your Lord is coming.' Mark 13:35 Watch therefore, for you do not know when the master of the house is coming—in the evening, at midnight, at the crowing of the rooster, or in the morning—

Mark 13:36 **lest, coming suddenly, he find you sleeping.**

Mark 13:37 "And what I say to you, **I say to all: Watch!"**

Besides these signs, I personally observed another sign, which I will share with you in this article. I am going to record it here, to admonish you, that you urgently prepare for the return of The Living Jesus Christ, because He is retuning soon, in the next few years, and He is returning very angry, followed by his Heavenly armies, to fight Satan, and all of Satan's present Satanic governments, Satan's kingdoms, and their armies. It is going to be a very great war, the greatest ever war, because it is fought by the Heavenly armies, which will be led by Jesus Christ Himself, as written in Revelation 19:14. And the armies in heaven, clothed in fine linen, white and clean, followed Him on white horses.

Revelation 19:15 Now out of His mouth goes a sharp sword, that with it He should strike the nations.

The following is written as a warning of what to do when Jesus Christ returns in anger: Isaiah 2:10 Enter into the rock, and hide in the dust, From the terror of the Lord and the glory of His majesty.

The coming battle is going to take place in the valley of Armageddon near Jerusalem, as written in Revelation 16:15: "Behold, I am coming as a thief. Blessed is he who watches, and keeps his garments, lest he walk naked and they see his shame."

Revelation 16:16 And they gathered them together, to the place called in Hebrew, Armageddon. Revelation 14:20 And the winepress was trampled outside the city, and blood came out of the winepress, up to the horses' bridles, for one thousand six hundred furlongs. That's a lot of blood, at least one meter, or 39 inches of blood high.

We find that the Apostle Paul was sentenced to appear in court in Rome, as recorded in the book of Acts. As recorded in the book of Acts 25:12, while sailing to get there, God created a very great storm, and the ship on which Paul was chained got shipwrecked on the small Island of Malta. God needed the Apostle Paul to stay on the small Island of Malta for several reasons that all fit into the Living Creator God's plan, which I will shortly explain.

God required the Apostle Paul to stay in Malta for a short while to fulfill the mission of the Living Creator God. The Living Creator God had to create a great tempest to destroy the ship on which Paul was a prisoner and chained, so Paul would have no transport left and would have to stay in Malta for a short while. If the ship had not been destroyed, the Apostle Paul would have stayed chained on the ship and not put his feet on the Island of Malta. If the ship the Apostle Paul was chained to was still capable of sailing, the moment the tempest stopped, the ship would have sailed away without Paul setting foot on the island of Malta.

Stopping on the Island of Malta was not on Paul's itinerary, but the Living Creator God wanted Paul to stop on the Island of Malta. Paul had no intention to stop in Malta. the Living Creator God was leading Paul to do the Living Creator God's will on the islands of Malta. I will write this episode of the Apostle Paul's shipwreck in great detail.

Here is how it happened: - Acts 27:13 When the south wind blew softly, supposing that they had obtained their desire, putting out to sea, they sailed close by Crete. Acts 27:14 But not long after, a tempestuous head wind arose, called Euroclydon, meaning a cyclonic tempestuous northeast wind, which blows in the Mediterranean, mostly in autumn and winter.

Acts 27:16 And running under the shelter of an island called Clauda, we secured the skiff with difficulty.

Acts 27:18 And because we were exceedingly tempest-tossed, the next day they lightened the ship.

Acts 27:19 On the third day, we threw the ship's tackle overboard with our own hands.

Acts 27:20 Now, when neither sun nor stars appeared for many days, and no small tempest beat on us, all hope that we would be saved was finally given up.

Acts 27:21 But after long abstinence from food, then Paul stood in the midst of them and said, "Men, you should have listened to me, and not have sailed from Crete and incurred this disaster and loss.

Acts 27:22 And now I urge you to take heart, for there will be no loss of life among you, but only of the ship.

Acts 27:23 For there stood by me this night an angel of God to whom I belong and whom I serve.

Acts 27:24 saying, 'Do not be afraid, Paul; you must be brought before Caesar; and indeed God has granted you all those who sail with you.'

Again, for the sake of one Godly man, all those on the ship were saved alive, two hundred and seventy-six persons on the ship. And again, for the sake of a very few elect of the Living Creator God, Jesus Christ, is cutting short the ruling time of Satan, and is coming to save this planet before Satan completely destroys this planet, with all humanity. Matthew 24:22 And unless those days were shortened, no flesh would be saved; (ALIVE) but for the elect's sake those days will be shortened.

Acts 27:25 Therefore, take heart, men, for I believe God that it will be just as it was told me.

Acts 27:26 However, we must run aground on a certain island." And that Island happened to be the Island of Malta.

Acts 27:27 Now, when the fourteenth night had come, as we were driven up and down in the Adriatic Sea, about midnight, the sailors sensed that they were drawing near some land.

Acts 27:28 And they took soundings and found it to be twenty fathoms; and when they had gone a little farther, they took soundings again and found it to be fifteen fathoms.

Acts 27:29 Then, fearing lest we should run aground on the rocks, they dropped four anchors from the stern, and prayed for day to come.

Acts 27:30 And as the sailors were seeking to escape from the ship, when they had let down the skiff into the sea, under pretense of putting out anchors from the prow,

Act 27:31 Paul said to the centurion and the soldiers, "Unless these men stay in the ship, you cannot be saved."

I am recording this in great length, and in detail, as it happened, to show you how the Living Creator God sometimes uses his messengers, and sometimes God's messengers are to overcome some very difficult situations, and are put to the limit, to test them to accomplish what the Living Creator God wants them to do. I visited the beach many times, where the Apostle Paul was shipwrecked. I used to go fishing with my fishing rod, in that same area, when I worked for the Maltese Government service system for six years.

Acts 27:32 Then the soldiers cut away the ropes of the skiff and let it fall off.

Acts 27:33 And as day was about to dawn, Paul implored them all to take food, saying, "Today is the fourteenth day you have waited and continued without food, and eaten nothing.

Acts 27:34 Therefore, I urge you to take nourishment, for this is for your survival, since not a hair will fall from the head of any of you."

Acts 27:35 And when he had said these things, he took bread and gave thanks to God in the presence of them all; and when he had broken it, he began to eat.

Acts 27:36 Then they were all encouraged, and also took food themselves.

Acts 27:37 And in all, we were two hundred and seventy-six persons on the ship.

Acts 27:38 So when they had eaten enough, they lightened the ship and threw out the wheat into the sea.

Acts 27:39 When it was day, they did not recognize the land; but they observed a bay with a beach, onto which they planned to run the ship if possible.

Acts 27:40 And they let go the anchors and left them in the sea, meanwhile losing the rudder ropes; and they hoisted the mainsail to the wind and made for shore.

This is correct; they left the 4 anchors in the sea because the 4 anchors were found outside the bay of Saint Thomas Bay, by Maltese divers, not very far from Munxar Reef. All four anchors were recovered, and the anchors are now preserved in the Maritime Museum in Malta.

Acts 27:41 But striking a place where two seas met, they ran the ship aground; and the prow stuck fast and remained immovable, but the stern was being broken up by the violence of the waves.

Between the two bays, there is a shallow reef, called MUNXAR REEF, only a few   from the water surface, and this is the reef onto which the prow of the ship hit and got stuck. St Thomas Sandy beach is still there, and the sailors aimed the ship for it, but they did not see the MUNXAR REEF a few feet under the water surface, as you can see it in the photo here. MUNXAR is the Maltese word for a SAW.

This hidden reef separated the two inlets, and this is why it is written, Acts 27:41 But striking a place where two seas met,

You can see the sandy beach in the top left corner of this photo, as well as the underwater reef, known as Munxar Reef, which separates two bays where two seas meet.

Acts 27:42 And the soldiers' plan was to kill the prisoners, lest any of them should swim away and escape.

Acts 27:43 But the centurion, wanting to save Paul, kept them from their purpose, and commanded that those who could swim should jump overboard first and get to land.

This shows that the Apostle Paul was one of the prisoners, chained to the ship.

Acts 27:44 and the rest, some on boards and some on parts of the ship. And so it was that they all escaped safely to land.

Acts 28:1 Now, when they had escaped, they then found out that the island was called Malta.

Acts 28:2 And the natives showed us unusual kindness; for they kindled a fire and made us all welcome, because of the rain that was falling and because of the cold.

Acts 28:3 But when Paul had gathered a bundle of sticks and laid them on the fire, a viper came out because of the heat, and fastened on his hand.

From where did this bundle of sticks, which the Apostle Paul threw on the fire, come? Remember that it was raining, and wet sticks don't burn.

From this, I gather that the lifestyle and system on the Maltese Islands have remained unchanged for over two thousand years. When I was young, in the summer months, we would gather and bundle all the sticks we could find and store them in our barn, which was called **"QASBIJA BARN,"** a large storeroom for these bundles of firewood. We used to bake our bread once a week at the bakery located on our street. Each time we baked our bread at this bakery, every family would take three bundles of these fire sticks to the bakery to heat up the oven. That's how we baked our weekly bread.

The fishermen in St. Thomas Bay village, would have been also farmers, and when they saw those people wet, went to their **"QASBIJA BARN"** and brought their bundles of their fire sticks to make many large bonfires to warm up the survivors of the shipwreck, and to warm up two hundred and seventy-six wet persons, the Maltese had to make lots of fire.

Lifestyle in Malta had never changed until I was young. I still remember a family in our village that was still living in a cave in one of the cliffs. Now in Malta, it is different altogether. The young generation living in Malta doesn't know the lifestyle of their past generations.

Acts 28:4 So when the natives saw the creature hanging from his hand, they said to one another, "No doubt this man is a murderer, whom, though he has escaped the sea, yet justice does not allow to live." **Acts 28:5** But he shook off the creature into the fire and suffered no harm.

It was the year 60 A.D. in the month of February when all this was happening. And I know how cold and windy February can be, because I was born on one of the Maltese Islands of Malta, called Gozo. Sometimes, with the cold, our teeth tap against the lower jaw with the upper jaw.

Acts 28:6 However, they were expecting that he would swell up or suddenly fall down dead. But after they had looked for a long time and saw no harm come to him, they changed their minds and said that he was a god.

This shows that a bite from these snakes is often fatal. This also shows me that the Maltese of 60 A.D. and beyond always had some strong religious beliefs in some gods. We still have many temples standing on the Maltese Islands, dating back thousands of years, which were dedicated to various gods.

Here is one of them called **"Ggantija Temple"**

Acts 28:7 In that region, there was an estate of the leading citizen of the island, whose name was Publius, who received us and entertained us courteously for three days. Acts 28:8 And it happened that the father of Publius lay sick of a fever and dysentery. Paul went into him and prayed, and he laid his hands on him and healed him.

Acts 28:9 So when this was done, the rest of those on the island who had diseases, also came and were healed.

Acts 28:10 They also honored us in many ways; and when we departed, they provided such things as were necessary.

The same snake from which Paul was bitten, which was a black, deadly snake, killed instantly, because, as it is recorded here, the onlookers expected the Apostle Paul to instantly drop dead when the snake bit him. Those black snakes still exist on the Maltese Islands, and as young children, we used to play with them. And we used to catch them while the snakes basked in the summer sun on the boundary walls of our fields. Tradition holds that Paul cursed the snakes in Malta, and as a result, they lost their venom.

I would like to write more about the Shipwreck of the Apostle Paul, which occurred at St. Thomas Bay on the Island of Malta. The Maltese People say and believe that the shipwreck of the Apostle Paul happened at St. Paul's Bay, which is another one of Satan's blatant LIES. Recently, it has been discovered and proven that the shipwreck happened at St. Thomas Bay, and even the four anchors were found at St. Thomas Bay and are on display in the Maritime Museum in Malta.

At St Paul's bay area the water is shallow, and does not register the depth recorded just before the ship broke into pieces, as recorded in, **Acts 27:28** And they took soundings and found it to be twenty fathoms;

Twenty Fathoms is approximately 120 feet, and in the area of St. Paul's bay, there is nowhere to be found this dept of water. From what I understand, this place, where this beach is called, St. Paul's bay, is maybe where the Apostle Paul stopped to preach the Gospel of the Kingdom of God, while he was on his way to visit the Island of Gozo. And the local Maltese people who lived in that village, named the place in the Apostle Paul's name. This is exactly as; a small hill, in Gozo, where tradition as passed on by the word of mouth, says that the Apostle Paul preached the Gospel of the Kingdom of God, on this small hill, and it is still named "THE HILL OF THE APOSTLE PAUL" to this very day. And I will write more about this small hill a little later, in this book.

The Apostle Paul was one among the passengers, who were prisoners being shipped to face their sentences in the high court in Rome, to be sentenced by the Roman Emperor, Caesar, and the Apostle Paul appealed to be sentenced by Caesar, as written in Acts 25:11 I appeal to Caesar." Acts 25:12 To Caesar you shall go!"

I may need to elaborate on my references to clarify this subject for you.

All the prisoners were shackled with chains in the lower hull of the ship. The centurion on the ship had a hundred soldiers with him to guard the prisoners. He is called a centurion because he leads one hundred soldiers. The centurion's name was Julius. Acts 27:1 And when it was decided that we should sail to Italy, they delivered Paul and some other prisoners to one named Julius, a centurion of the Augustan Regiment. And Julius treated Paul kindly and gave him the liberty to go to his friends and receive care. The total number of persons on board the ship, as written in Acts 27:37, was two hundred and seventy-six persons. It was a large sailing ship with sails.

The author of the book of Acts, to my knowledge, was Luke, as mentioned in Colossians 4:14, who was also known as Luke the beloved physician. He was traveling to assist the Apostle Paul. The book of Acts is written with great detail and accuracy throughout. He provided very accurate details on everything, immersing the reader in the action, as if they were present at the event.

The Apostle Paul had some sort of disability, and needed assistance, and from what we can see, Luke being a physician, accompanied the Apostle Paul, on Paul's way to Rome. We read the following; 2Corinthians 12:7 And lest I should be exalted above measure by the abundance of the revelations, a thorn in the flesh was given to me, a messenger of Satan to buffet me, lest I be exalted above measure.

2Corinthians 12:8 Concerning this thing I pleaded with the Lord three times that it might depart from me.

2Co 12:9 And He said to me, "My grace is sufficient for you, for My strength is made perfect in weakness." Therefore most gladly I will rather boast in my infirmities, that the power of Christ may rest upon me.

From this we learn that sometimes we don't receive what we request and ask for every time.

Acts 27:40 And they let go of the anchors and left them in the sea. The four anchors were all still in the water and were discovered by Maltese divers off St. Thomas Bay. They are now all on display at the Maritime Museum in Malta.

When the ship ran aground, the soldiers planned to kill all the chained prisoners, but Julius, the centurion, wanted to save the Apostle Paul, as written in **Acts 27:42** . And the soldiers' plan was to kill the prisoners, lest any of them should swim away and escape.

Acts 27:43 But the centurion, wanting to save Paul, kept them from their purpose.

This shipwreck occurred in February 60 A.D., a time when February is typically a very cold month in Malta. All those two hundred and seventy-six persons had wet clothes on them. Around

St. Thomas Bay was a small fishing village at that time, and all the people went out to help those who were on the ship. They took with them bundles of firewood sticks, which they had stored in their barns to use for their baking of their bread, at the local bakery, and the Maltese made big bonfires to warm up, and to make dry all those who survived the shipwreck, as written in Acts 28:2 And the natives showed us unusual kindness; for they kindled a fire and made us all welcome, because of the rain that was falling and because of the cold. (Very Accurate Recording by the Author) The Maltese went far beyond the needs of the survivors.

The Apostle Paul was throwing one of those bundles of firewood when the viper bit his hand, Acts 28:3 . But when Paul had gathered a bundle of sticks and laid them on the fire, a viper came out because of the heat and fastened on his hand. The viper was so deadly that it killed the victim instantly, as written in Acts 28:6 . However, they were expecting that he would swell up or suddenly fall down dead. But after they had looked for a long time and saw no harm come to him, they changed their minds and said that he was a god.

The last verse reveals that the Maltese of 60 A.D. were religious people, believers in the gods. Even before Noah's floods, when the entire world was considered evil, those living in Malta had many temples dedicated to their gods. This is evident in the massive Rock Temples that still stand in Malta to this day, as I previously showed.

The Maltese system has not changed to this very day, because every city and every village in Malta has very strong beliefs, devotions, and Traditions, with many temples dedicated to their area's patronage deity. And in the summer months, the Maltese people carry their deities on their shoulders through their cities and villages, accompanied by loud music, bands playing marches, and colossal displays of very expensive fireworks.

To put it simply, the devotions and Traditions to their gods in Malta have remained unchanged for many thousands of years since the first settlers arrived. Perhaps the Apostle Paul introduced them to the True Living Creator God and His Gospel message, which included the coming Kingdom of God, but they unfortunately reverted to their old traditions, devotions, and customs, which they still practice to this very day.

Unfortunately, the entire world doesn't know what they are worshipping and giving their honor to. I feel sorry for the people because they lack knowledge and don't know what they are doing, as written in Hosea 4:6 My people are destroyed for lack of knowledge. Because you have rejected knowledge,

Satan has deceived all of mankind with his lies. Only when Jesus Christ returns and removes Satan will people start to see their mistakes of worship and venerating idols and images, violating the **TEN COMMANDMENTS.** The second Commandment says not to worship images and idols of any kind.

2nd Commandment: - Exodus 20:4 "You shall not make for yourself a carved image--any likeness of anything that is in heaven above, or that is in the earth beneath, or that is in the water under the earth; 5 you shall not bow down to them nor serve them. For I, the Lord your God, am a jealous God, visiting the iniquity of the fathers upon the children to the third and fourth generations of those who hate Me, 6 but showing mercy to thousands, to those who love Me and keep My commandments."

Worshipping idols is breaking the Second Commandment, and breaking one commandment, the Apostle James says, James 2:10 For whoever shall keep the whole law, and yet stumble in one point, he is guilty of all. James 2:11 For He who said, **"DO NOT COMMIT ADULTERY,"** also said, **"DO NOT MURDER."**

Worshiping of idols, and with their idols carried on their shoulders, goes back thousands of years, and we have record of what I am writing as written in, Isaiah 46:6 They lavish gold out of the bag, And weigh silver on the scales; They hire a goldsmith, and he makes it a god; They prostrate themselves, yes, they worship.

Isaiah 46:7 They bear it on the shoulder, they carry it, and set it in its place, and it stands; From its place it shall not move.

Though one cries out to it, yet it cannot answer nor save him out of his trouble. Isaiah 46:8 "Remember this, and show yourselves men; Recall to mind, O you transgressors.

Psalms 115:4 Their idols are silver and gold, the work of men's hands. Psalms 115:5 They have mouths, but they do not speak; Eyes they have, but they do not see; Psalms 115:6 They have ears, but they do not hear; Noses they have, but they do not smell; Psalms 115:7 They have hands, but they do not handle; Feet they have, but they do not walk; Nor do they mutter through their throat. Psalms 115:8 Those who make them are like them; So is everyone who trusts in them. Psalms 135:15 The idols of the nations are silver and gold, the work of men's hands.

HERE IS ONE EXAMPLE of what I am writing about.

111

Worshipping of Idols is breaking **THE TEN COMMANDMENTS.**

The worship of Idols is being loyal and doing the service of Satan. One cannot serve the Living Creator God while doing Satan's service. Jesus Christ said, as written in Matthew 6:24, "No one can serve two masters; for either he will hate the one and love the other, or else he will be loyal to the one and despise the other. You cannot serve God and mammon.

All those who break **THE TEN COMMANDMENTS ARE LOVING SATAN.**

Jesus Christ said as written in John 14:15, "If you love Me, keep My commandments." 1 John 5:3 For this is the love of God, that we keep His commandments. And His commandments are not burdensome.

2 John 1:6 This is love, that we walk according to His commandments. This is the commandment, that as you have heard from the beginning, you should walk in it.

In the next few years, two prophets of the Living Creator God will be preaching the True Gospel of The Kingdom of the Living Creator God, to the entire world, as written in the Book of Revelation, and I always wonder how the people are going to react to the messages that these two prophets are going to preach to the world, while the entire world is adhering to their beliefs, traditions and their customs.

People are not going to like them, because in the end, the two prophets of the Living Creator God are going to be killed as written in Revelation 11:7. When they finish their testimony, the beast that ascends out of the bottomless pit will make war against them, overcome them, and kill them.

A GIVEN SIGN OF THE RETURN OF JESUS CHRIST

In Malta, up to the early 1900s, few Maltese people could read and write, and information was passed down through word of mouth from one generation to the next for many thousands of years. Even when I was young, I remember the summer nights, when at sunset, a whole street gathered at one place, mostly on a wheat trashing floor, lying down on the hay stack, enjoying the summer nights cool breeze, after they had dinner, with a glass of home brew red wine, and they recite what they heard and what was passed on to them, by their older people, the generation before them. I still remember many of their old yarns, and I will mention one of them here, which fits perfectly with what I am writing about. I heard them say the following many times over: "The end of this age will be in the year two thousand and a few years after that." This was in the mid-1950s, when I used to listen to the old people lying down on the haystacks and hear them say that so many times. Now, based on my knowledge of this subject, they were completely correct. Additionally, the old tales claimed that when the Apostle Paul was bitten by a viper, all the black vipers on the Maltese Islands lost their venom.

Tradition says that the Apostle Paul visited the three main islands, including Gozo, where I was born, and he healed everyone who came to him seeking healing. When we read all the letters that the Apostle Paul wrote, he consistently prioritized his

114

teachings regarding the return of Jesus Christ, who would come down from heaven to establish His Father's kingdom on earth. Paul's Gospel teaching was the same Gospel message that Jesus Christ gave to the people, and preached, as written in Matthew 4:23. And Jesus went about all Galilee, teaching in their synagogues, **preaching the gospel of the kingdom,** and healing all kinds of sickness and all kinds of disease among the people.

This was the same main message that both the Apostle Paul and Jesus Christ conveyed during their lifetimes, and I am convinced and believe that Jesus Christ will return in the next few years to establish the Kingdom of His Father here on earth. Jesus Christ will have a very simple message to live by, along with simple rules outlined in the Ten Commandments and the Kingdom of God. The Apostle Paul frequently mentions the Kingdom of God in his letters.

Now is the time, that I will give you, the reader, the reason, why I am sure that the return of Jesus Christ, of Him coming down from Heaven, as King of Kings, is very close, with only now a few more years, from, that we can count the coming years that are left, on our hands fingers, without including any of our toes, as written in 1Timothy 6:14 that you keep this commandment without spot, blameless until our Lord Jesus Christ's appearing, 1Timothy 6:15 which He will manifest in His own time, He who is the blessed and only Potentate, the **King of kings** and Lord of Lords, Revelation 19:16 And He has on His robe and on His thigh a name written: **KING OF KINGS AND LORD OF LORDS.**

When I was young, during the hot summer season in the Maltese Islands, my father would take us swimming in a place near where we lived, not far, less than two kilometers away, near a natural window of 35 meters high, known as the Azure Window. This Azure Window was well known around the world. It was highly advertised for the tourists. This magnificent window attracted visitors from around the world, particularly from Europe. It was one of the main attractions for millions of visitors in the summer months, who visited the historical Islands of Malta. The Azure Window is renowned worldwide for its unique and significant features.

What I am about to write for you may seem unconvincing to you, but please consider what I have to say. I forgive you if you do that, because I know that what you are reading here in this article will all be fulfilled, within the lifespan of most of you. The Apostle Peter wrote about this scoffing, a long time ago, because I know that we are living in the last few years, of this present age, ruled by Satan, under whom the entire world is following, with everyone being deceived, and everyone is suffering, one way or another, and not knowing another way of life, except a life of sorrow and pain, crying, and deaths, as written in 2 Peter

3:3 knowing this first: that scoffers will come in the last days, walking according to their own lusts,

2 Peter 3:4and saying, "Where is the promise of His coming? For since the fathers fell asleep, all things continue as they were from the beginning of creation."

Revelation 12:9 So the great dragon was cast out, that serpent of old, called the Devil and **Satan, who deceives the whole world;** he was cast to the earth, and his angels were cast out with him. Revelation 20:2 He laid hold of the dragon, that serpent of old, who is the Devil and Satan, and bound him for a thousand years;

Revelation 20:3 and he cast him into the bottomless pit, and shut him up, and set a seal on him, **so that he should deceive the nations no more** till the thousand years were finished. But after these things, he must be released for a little while.

Yes, unfortunately, Satan is ruling this entire world, and everyone is deceived by Satan, whether you believe it or not. Satan is very powerful, so powerful that he attempted and thought that he could overthrow the throne of the Living Creator God. Revelation 12:7 And war broke out in heaven: Michael and his angels fought with the dragon; and the dragon and his angels fought.

Revelation 12:8, but they did not prevail, nor was a place found for them in heaven any longer.

Don't think that when Satan tempted Eve, he turned into an ugly-looking snake. He would have appeared to Eve as a beautiful, attractive angel of light, as he still does to this very time, in many places around the world, to deceive whole nations, as written in 2Corinthians 11:14 . And no wonder! For Satan himself transforms himself into an angel of light.

To this very day, we see many apparitions of appearances of Satan in many places around the earth, appearing in many different shapes and forms, of men and women.

Satan discerns the time in which we are living now. He knows that his time is nearly up, and that he will be judged and sentenced, and locked up for one thousand years. Satan knows all this. He even knows the year of his judgment time. He is going to become very angry, and he will do all he can to destroy the planet Earth before his time is up. This is the reason why God has to cut Satan's time short, as Jesus Christ confirms this, as written in Matthew 24:22 And unless those days were shortened, no flesh would be saved; (ALIVE) but for the elect's sake those days will be shortened.

The Apostle Peter wrote the following for our time now as written in 2Peter 3:1 Beloved, I now write to you this second epistle (in both of which I stir up your pure minds by way of reminder), 2Peter 3:2 that you may be mindful of the words which were spoken before by the holy prophets, and of the commandment of us, the apostles of the Lord and Savior.

Unfortunately, things are unlikely to remain the same for much longer. In the near future, we can expect significant changes for the worse. Satan is going to cause havoc on this whole planet, and calculations show that only ten percent (10 %) will be left alive, from all of us humans, by the time Satan is locked up for one thousand years, by the returned Jesus Christ. I will provide proof of this later in the article.

Now we turn to the most visited place, by millions of foreign tourists who visit Malta in the summer months, to the place where my father used to take us swimming in the hot summer months on the Island of Gozo, one of the Maltese Islands.

<*> - - - The AZURE WINDOW ON THE ISLAND OF GOZO - MALTA - WAS CREATED BY GOD - **TO BE A SIGN FOR OUR END TIME NOW** - - - <*>

I happened to be born near where this remarkable Azure Window was located. I was predestinated from before the foundation of the world, Ephesians 1:4, to be born at this special place, to be able to know what I am conveying to you in this writing. Ephesians 1:4 just as He chose us in Him before the foundation of the world. Ephesians 1:11 In Him also we have obtained an inheritance, being predestined according to the purpose of Him.

Nobody else knows what I know, about why this great window was created by the Living Creator God, to serve its purpose, and when that purpose was fulfilled, and came to pass, it got swallowed by the sea in a matter of a few seconds.

This was the reason I was born in this special place: to pass on to you the purpose of the creation of the Azure Window, which was on the blueprint of the Living Creator God, from before His creation of the entire universe.

<*> - - - Here I will insert a photo of The AZURE WINDOW AS IT LOOKED FROM CREATION - - - <*> until the late 1950s and early 1960s, and this AZURE WINDOW was still the same as when the Apostle Paul looked at it, in 60 AD. This photo was taken in the late 1950s A.D. This Azure Window was still solid, in the same state as when it was created. - What would you have thought and said if you were told in the 1950s that one day the sea would swallow it, when it looked like this? - - - <*>

YOU WOULD HAVE LAUGHED, AND THOUGHT THAT IT WAS A JOKE, WHAT YOU JUST HEARD.

The Azure Window was located on the west side of the island of Gozo. It was created by the Living Creator God, from the very beginning of the creation of this planet earth, to be a mark and to be a sign, declaring the end of this present age, under the rule of Satan, as I am going to describe to you shortly.

The Living Creator God can declare the end from the very beginning. As written earlier, the Living Creator God prepares the end from the beginning. God created the Azure Window from the beginning to be a witness for our time. Isaiah 48:3 "I have declared the former things from the beginning; They went forth from My mouth, and I caused them to hear it. Suddenly, I did them, and they came to pass.

During the summer months, when I was in my early teenage years, I used to go fishing from the top of this Azure Window. I always returned home loaded with fish. When I arrived home, I would kindle a fire on the street, and when the fire died down and turned to charcoal, we would place the fish on the hot charcoal and eat them. Four to five families would gather together in our street around a hot charcoal fire. Each one of us had a deep plate with olive oil, vinegar, salt and pepper, and taking the cooked fish from the top of the charcoal, and dipping the cooked fish in the plate, we used to have a good lunch or evening meal, with the fresh fish, which I used to catch, from the top of that Azure Window, when I was in my early teenager years.

This is the type of fishing baskets and Traps that I fished with from the top of the Azure Window.

The traps used to have a ball of fish food hanging in the fishing basket, as shown in this photo, releasing small fragments of fish food. The fish would enter the fishing basket from underneath to feed, and then get trapped inside.

You can see the fish in these two fishing baskets.

I have video clips of people jumping 35 meters from the top of this Azure Window.

My father never let us jump that high.

We used to swim here very often in the summer months.

The Azure Window was 32 meters high and remained unchanged from Its Creation to the 1950s, when this photo was taken, and when we swam near it in the summer months. God had this window in mind when He created it, for a specific reason: to serve its purpose, to serve as a sign, to show me that the end of this age is coming to a close and will soon come to an end, and that the return of Jesus Christ is imminent.

One of the commissions that the Apostle Paul was assigned to do, besides bringing the Gospel message of the coming Kingdom of The Living Creator God, to the Maltese Islands, was also to point his finger at this great Azure Window, and mark it, to be a sign, for us at this time now, that the timeframe of Satan's rule, over this entire planet is coming to an end, and that

123

the return of Jesus Christ is near. I may be the only one with this knowledge, which I am sharing with you here. I am not aware of any others with this knowledge. The Living Creator God wants me to share this knowledge with the world, so that people will be warned of the perilous times in which we live.

In the near future, a few more years from now, there is going to be famines, nuclear wars, burning entire large cities around the world, deadly diseases, and contagious deadly viruses. Wake up, people, because the time of sorrows is coming, and we are going to live through them.

FAMINE WILL TRIGGER CANNIBALISM - Deuteronomy 28:53 You shall eat the fruit of your own body, the flesh of your sons and your daughters whom the LORD your God has given you, in the siege and desperate straits in which your enemy shall distress you. Deuteronomy 28:56 The tender and delicate woman among you, who would not venture to set the sole of her foot on the ground because of her delicateness and sensitivity, will refuse to the husband of her bosom, and to her son and her daughter, Deuteronomy 28:57 her placenta which comes out from between her feet and her children whom she bears; for she will eat them secretly for lack of everything.

Isaiah 1:7 Your country is desolate, **your cities are burned with fire.**

This photo of the Azure Window was taken in the 1970s. Here is where my father used to take us swimming. My Father used to tell us, "Look closely at this great window, because one day it will disappear, and the sea will swallow it." I recall asking my father, "Why, Dad?" My father used to answer me, "I always heard my ancestors saying that when this window is swallowed by the sea, the time will be very close to the end of this age, and the return of Jesus Christ will be near." I used to ask my father, "How did your ancestors know this, about this large window?" My father used to make us turn a 180 degrees back, and he used to point to a small hill, at a distance of about two kilometers, and say to us, "You see that little hill up there, in the distance, the name of that hill is **"THE HILL OF THE APOSTLE PAUL,"** my father used to bring me here, swimming in the summer months,

125

and used to tell me, that, the old people used to say, that the Apostle Paul preached the Gospel to some people who lived up there, on that small hill. The people who lived up there asked the Apostle Paul, when the end of this age will come. Then the Apostle Paul pointed his finger to this large window, and told the people who lived up there, that when this window is swallowed by the sea, the time of the end of this age has come very close, and Jesus Christ will be coming soon."

I have provided you with all the necessary information about the return of Jesus Christ, so that this upcoming event will not take you by surprise, like a snare catching its victim unaware. I have made you aware to prepare yourself for what is coming, in the not-too-distant future. Luke_21:35

This is the place where my father always took us swimming, in this beautiful blue water. This photo was taken in the late 1990s. From this photo, we can see that the top layer of this window is crumbling rapidly. What a contrast compared to the photo of how this great window looked when it was created, and as it appeared when the photo was taken in the 1950s, as I previously showed you.

Looking through the Azure Window, towards the small hill, still called to this day, the hill of the Apostle Paul, upon which the Apostle Paul preached. We can see the hill from where the Apostle Paul pointed his finger towards this window in 60 AD.

Now you can see how my father plainly passed on to us what he heard from his ancestors say about this great window. That hill that we can see through this Azure Window carries a lot of history. Now you can see how the Apostle Paul pointed his finger from that small hill, directly to this Azure Window. In the mid 1950's foundations of houses were discovered on that small hill, which confirms that some people lived there, at some time, and also confirms what my father's ancestors, passed on from generation to generation, by the word of mouth, of what took place on that small hill in 60 AD, when people lived on that hill.

I visited this same place, in the summer of 2019, and the great Azure Window was nowhere to be seen. It was swallowed by the sea at 9:40 a.m. on Wednesday, March 8, 2017, and nobody was hurt by its destruction. When this happened, it was worldwide news. God wanted the entire world to learn about and know the destruction of the Azure Window. Every event has a reason for its occurrence. The events connected to this Azure Window prove to me that the time of the return of Jesus Christ, to come down from Heaven, to save His creation, is very close. Unless the time of Satan's ruling kingdom is cut short, nothing that breathes will be left alive, as written in Matthew 24:21 For then there will be great tribulation, such as has not been since the beginning of the world until this time, no, nor ever shall be. Matthew 24:22 And unless those days were shortened, no flesh would be saved; (ALIVE) but for the elect's sake, those days will be shortened.

Now another thought comes to my mind, and I will share it with you here. We find written in Matthew 24:18, when the disciples asked Jesus about the signs of the end of this age. It is important that I bring it to your attention.

Matthew 24:1 Then Jesus went out and departed from the temple, and His disciples came up to show Him the buildings of the temple.

Matthew 24:2 And Jesus said to them, "Do you not see all these things? Assuredly, I say to you, not one stone shall be left here upon another, that shall not be thrown down."

We find here that Jesus Christ, just as the Apostle Paul, pointed His finger towards the building of the Temple in Jerusalem in the same way as the Apostle Paul pointed his finger towards the Azure Window. Here, Jesus Christ is telling them that the destruction of the Temple will be one of the signs. Sure enough, not one single stone was left upon another, because when the Temple got burned down, all the gold that covered the inside walls got melted like water and went between the stones, right down to the very foundations. People unearthed the foundations to get the melted gold from between the stones. The people left no stone unturned. Therefore, just as the prophecy of the Apostle Paul came to pass, so did Jesus Christ's prophecy. Matthew 24:2 And Jesus said to them, "Do you not see all these things? Assuredly, I say to you, not one stone shall be left here upon another, that shall not be thrown down."

Matthew 24:3 Now as He sat on the Mount of Olives, the disciples came to Him privately, saying, "Tell us, when will these things be? And what will be the sign of Your coming, **and of the end of the age?"**

The Disciples wanted to know when Jesus Christ would return to establish His Father's Kingdom on this earth.

Matthew 24:7 For nation will rise against nation, and kingdom against kingdom. And there will be famines, pestilences, and earthquakes in various places.

Matthew 24:8 **All these are the beginning of sorrows.**

I want to bring to your attention that we are living at the end of this age, which is ruled by Satan, and we are witnessing all these end-time signs, which Jesus Christ told His disciples, all around us. We should not ignore them.

We are witnessing wars in every corner of the world. We are witnessing all different types of viruses, pestilences, and many massive earthquakes. Jesus Christ also mentions **FAMINES**. Famine means shortages of food. All this also means that during the coming years, we are going to experience years of distress, for all of us, because of Satan's anger, as written in Revelation 12:12 "Therefore, rejoice, O heavens, and you who dwell in them! **Woe to the inhabitants of the earth** and the sea! For the devil has come down to you, having great wrath, because he knows that he has a short time."

A WARNING: - There is going to be an escalation of what I had just recorded here.

Satan is going to smash this planet Earth, in the few years he has left, before he is thrown into prison for one thousand years. And he knows that his time is short. He is going to act like some tenants who smash the house they rented, and lived in it for a long time, and when they are being evicted it, they smash it before they leave. We can expect some very difficult years ahead of us, just before the return of Jesus Christ, when He comes down from Heaven to save us. I am expecting a great destruction of this entire planet. Many people are going to die, and only a very few people are going to be left alive.

In the same way, as we saw the rapid deterioration and crumbling of the Azure Window, falling apart until the sea swallowed it, this is also showing us how fast the deterioration condition of this planet Earth is going to take place, when Satan starts to destroy this Earth, in the near future. It will be a **SUDDEN,** quick, and rapid destruction. The sudden destruction of this planet by Satan would not be expected. Many would expect it to occur in the same manner as it did during Noah's flood. And as it was with the destruction of Sodom, as written in Luke 21:34, "But take heed to yourselves, lest your hearts be weighed down with carousing, drunkenness, and cares of this life, and that Day come on you unexpectedly.

Luke 21:35 **For it will come as a snare** on all those who dwell on the face of the whole earth. A snare will catch its victim unaware.

Luke 17:26 And as it was in the days of Noah, so it will be also in the days of the Son of Man:

Luke 17:27 They ate, they drank, they married wives, they were given in marriage, until the day that Noah entered the ark, and the flood came and destroyed them all.

Luke 17:28 Likewise, as it was also in the days of Lot: They ate, they drank, they bought, they sold, they planted, they built.

Luke 17:29 But on the day that Lot went out of Sodom, it rained fire and brimstone from heaven and destroyed them all.

Luke 17:30 Even so will it be in the day when the Son of Man is revealed.

WARNING: - Nuclear wars are going to burn up parts of this planet, and billions of people are going to be burned alive.

I am writing all this for you, to warn you ahead of time, just before the coming great destruction. Please pay attention to what you are reading here, and take heed, to be prepared, for what we will soon be going through - **a very difficult time. You are being warned, you are left without an excuse, and in the end, you will not be able to say that you were not warned.**

According to the written, **TRUE Word of the Living Creator God**, by the time of the return of Jesus Christ, coming down from Heaven to save mankind, only ten percent of the present population, will be left alive, 90% of the present population are going to die, and will not be here, as written in Isaiah 6:11 Then I said, "Lord, how long?" And He answered: "Until the cities are laid waste and without inhabitant, The houses are without a man, The land is utterly desolate."

Isaiah 6:12 The LORD has removed men far away, And the forsaken places are many in the midst of the land.

Isaiah 6:13 **But yet a tenth will be in it,** And will return and be for consuming, As a terebinth tree or as an oak, Whose stump remains when it is cut down. So the holy seed shall be its stump." The Holy seed is the Elect mentioned in Matthew 24:22.

The Tenth will be preserved and left alive to replenish the human population for one thousand years, under the rule of Jesus Christ.

God is preserving one-tenth of the entire present population. Every tenth from everything, including humanity, is holy to God. Leviticus 27:32 And concerning the tithe of the herd or the flock, of whatever passes under the rod, **the tenth one shall be holy to the LORD.**

The sheep that are counted coming out of the barn, nine WILL go to the slaughter, and the tenth sheep is saved. Jesus Christ is coming to save His creation, before the total destruction made by Satan. If Jesus Christ does not return on time, this planet will disappear like the Azure Window, which disappeared **IN A VERY SHORT PERIOD OF TIME.**

We find written more about the one-tenth to be saved alive, as written in Ezekiel 5:1: "And you, son of man, take a sharp sword, take it as a barber's razor, and pass it over your head and your beard; then take scales to weigh and divide the hair.

Ezekiel 5:2 You shall **burn with fire one-third** in the midst of the city, when the days of the siege are finished; then you shall take **one-third and strike around it with the sword,** and **one-third you shall scatter in the wind**: I will draw out a sword after them.

Ezekiel 5:3 You shall also take a small number of them and bind them in the edge of your garment.

Regarding the one-third to be burned by fire, the Living Creator God inspired the prophet Malachi to write the following for us living at this time.

134

Malachi 4:1 Behold**, the day cometh, that shall burn as an oven**; and all the proud, yea, and all that do wickedly, shall be stubble: and the day that cometh shall burn them up, says the LORD of hosts, that it shall leave them neither root nor branch.

Atomic, Hydrogen, and vaporization warfare is predicted for the near future.

I like to ask a question. How many people are going to perish, from now in 2025 and another ten years from now?? I rely on the words spoken by Jesus Christ, as recorded in Luke 13:3. I tell you, no; but unless you repent, you will all likewise perish.

As I have already written, according to Scripture, 90% of the present population are going to perish, and the majority of those perishing are going to be men.

Why am I writing this??

The Holy Scripture, which is inspired to be written by the Living Creator God, shows me to write the following.

The god of this world, as written in 2 Corinthians 4:4, whose minds the god of this age has blinded, who do not believe.

The god of this present age, Satan, who tricked Eve in the Garden of Eden, snatched from Adam and Eve to rule this Planet for 120 Jubilee period of time, as written in Genesis 6:3 And the LORD said, "My Spirit shall not strive with man forever, for he is indeed flesh; yet his days shall be one hundred and twenty years."

135

The word years in the original is H8141. shânâh *shaw-neh', shaw-*
naw meaning a period of time.

A period of time can refer to a span of 49 years, encompassing one Jubilee period. And based on the Jubilee calendar, restored by Joseph Dumond at sightedmoon.com, we are in this last Jubilee, which is 120 jubilees since the creation of Adam. This present Jubilee will end in the year of 2044. I am basing this on the Jubilee Calendar from Joseph Dumond at sightedmoon.com. But Jesus Christ tells me that if Satan is allowed to rule this planet full-time, up to the year of 2044, everything that breathes air will perish, and to save humanity from total annihilation from Satan, the Living Creator God is going to cut short Satan's ruling, as I have already written earlier. I write it again here. Matthew 24:22 And unless those days were shortened, no flesh would be saved; but for the elect's sake those days will be shortened.

Jesus Christ is returning soon to cut short Satan's ruling of this planet, and He is returning very angry with His Heavenly Armies to fight the god of this age, Satan, and Satan's armies, as written in Revelation 19:11. Now I saw heaven opened, and behold, a white horse. And He who sat on him was called Faithful and True, and in righteousness He judges and makes war. Revelation 19:12 His eyes were like a flame of fire, and on His head were many crowns. He had a name written that no one knew except Himself.

Revelation 19:13 He was clothed with a robe dipped in blood, and His name is called The Word of God. Rev 19:14 And the armies in heaven, clothed in fine linen, white and clean, followed Him on white horses.

Did you read that Jesus Christ is returning angry to make war, with eyes that are angry and fiery?

I can write that, based on my mathematical knowledge of calculations, all will be fulfilled within less than ten years' time. And I am waiting for most of you reading this book to witness what I am writing here.

Satan knows the timing more than I or anybody else, the year and the month, of the return of Jesus Christ, to judge him, (SATAN) and put Satan in prison for one thousand years, as written in this book, Revelation 20:3.

Satan knows the year and the month of the return of Jesus Christ, but he does not know the day or the hour, as written in Matthew 24:36: "But of that day and hour no one knows, not even the angels of heaven, but My Father only.

Satan is going to prepare this world's armies in the valley of Megiddo to fight Jesus Christ and His armies as written in Revelation 16:13 . And I saw three unclean spirits like frogs coming out of the mouth of the dragon (Satan), out of the mouth of the beast, and out of the mouth of the false prophet. Revelation 16:14 For they are spirits of demons, performing signs, which go out to the kings of the earth and of the whole world, to gather them to the battle of that great day of God Almighty. Revelation

16:16 And they gathered them together to the place called in Hebrew, Armageddon.

Here I will insert, the Holy Scripture, which is written in the book of Revelation, to prove to you that the Book of Revelation was originally written by the Living God the Father Himself, Revelation 5:1 And I saw in the right hand of Him who sat on the throne a scroll written inside and on the back, sealed with seven seals.

Satan is going to gather and prepare the whole world's armies to confront the returned Jesus Christ and His Heavenly armies.

The World's armies, led by Satan are going to make war with Jesus Christ, as written in, Revelation 17:14 . These will make war with the Lamb, and the Lamb will overcome them, for He is Lord of lords and King of kings; and those who are with Him are called, chosen, and faithful."

The world's armies making war with the returned Jesus Christ are going to be dissolved into liquid blood as written in Revelation 14:20 . And the winepress was trampled outside the city, and blood came out of the winepress, up to the horses' bridles, for one thousand six hundred furlongs.

One thousand six hundred furlongs is a very long distance, and the horses' bridles will be a little bit more than three feet high from the ground. That is a mighty big pool of blood in the valley of Armageddon.

The armies gathered to fight Jesus Christ would start killing each other, and at the same time, they would be liquidated even while standing and walking. Zechariah 14:12 "And this shall be the plague with which **the Lord will strike all the people who fought against Jerusalem: Their flesh shall dissolve while they stand on their feet, Their eyes shall dissolve in their sockets, And their tongues shall dissolve in their mouths.** 13 It shall come to pass in that day that a great panic from the Lord will be among them. **Everyone will seize the hand of his neighbour, and raise his hand against his neighbour's hand."**

The enemies of Jesus Christ will be liquidated slowly into blood, and then their liquid will be burned like the fat of lambs into smoke. The birds will have enough time that afternoon to have their supper from the dissolving flesh of hundreds of millions of those gathered in the valley of Armageddon, to fight Jesus Christ. Evaporating the liquid blood into smoke with fire will clean up their blood. Psalm 37:20 But the wicked shall perish; and the enemies of the LORD, Like the splendor of the meadows, shall vanish. Into smoke they shall vanish away.

When the nations near and far hear what Jesus Christ has done to His gathered enemies, those still alive will know that Jesus Christ is the new World King and the True Living Creator God of Israel. Psalm 59:13 "Consume them in wrath, consume them that they may not be; and let them know that God rules in Jacob To the ends of the earth. Selah."

When the nations that gathered to make war against Jesus Christ are evaporated and consumed as if they have never existed, Satan with his demon angels are bound and put away for one thousand years, and Jesus Christ will be the new Living Creator God ruling this Planet Earth for one thousand years, until Satan is released from prison.

When Satan is released out of prison, he will again gather an army for a war against Jesus Christ in Jerusalem, as written in Revelation 20:7 Now when the thousand years have expired, Satan will be released from his prison Revelation 20:8 and will go out to deceive the nations which are in the four corners of the earth, Gog and Magog, to gather them together to battle, whose number is as the sand of the sea. Revelation 20:9 They went up on the breadth of the earth and surrounded the camp of the saints and the beloved city. And fire came down from God out of heaven and devoured them.

Then Satan and his demons are destroyed forever, and never to exist ever again, as written in Revelation 20:10 . The devil, who deceived them, was cast into the lake of fire and brimstone

I want remind the reader to know that when I quote the Book of Revelation, I want the reader to remember that the Book of Revelation was originally written by The Living God the Father of Jesus Christ, and Jesus Christ, got the Apostle John to pass the Book of Revelation on to us, as written in Revelation 1:1 The Revelation of Jesus Christ, which God gave Him to show His servants—things which must shortly take place. And He sent and signified it by His angel to His servant John.

After the reader of this book has read about the world's armies being destroyed by Jesus Christ in the valley of Megiddo, I want to highlight that the majority of the soldiers will be men, and there will be a scarcity of men left alive. And the Holy Scripture tells us and confirms this to us, as I am going to pass it on to the reader.

When all this has passed, men will be rarer than a bar of pure gold, as written in Isaiah 13:12 I will make a mortal, rarer than fine gold, A man more than the golden wedge of Ophir.

And this is going to happen when the Living Creator Jesus Christ returns to this earth in anger, as written in Isaiah 13:13 Therefore I will shake the heavens, And the earth will move out of her place, In the wrath of the LORD of hosts And in the day of His fierce anger.

Men will be so rare that seven women will take hold and live with one man, as written in Isaiah 4:1 And in that day seven women shall take hold of one man, saying, "We will eat our own food and wear our own apparel; Only let us be called by your name, To take away our reproach."

Jesus Christ was the One, called the Word, who created everything, as written in John 1:1 In the beginning was the Word, and the Word was with God, and the Word was God.

John 1:2 He was in the beginning with God. John 1:3 **All**

things were made through Him, and without Him nothing was made that was made. John 1:4 In Him was life, and the life was the light of men.

John 1:14 And the Word became flesh and dwelt among us, and we beheld His glory, the glory as of the only begotten of the Father, full of grace and truth.

John 17:5 And now, O Father, glorify Me together with Yourself, with the glory which I had with You before the world was.

Living under Satan's rule is living with Satan's lies, and the entire world is totally deceived and does not know it. By living in the soon coming Kingdom of God, the entire world will live under Jesus Christ rule, ruling this planet earth with the **TEN COMMANDMENTS,** the people will be living in the **TRUTH,** and by the **TRUTH,** because Jesus Christ is the **TRUTH,** as written in John 14:6 Jesus said to him, "**I am the way, the truth,** and the life. No one comes to the Father except through Me. As I wrote earlier, **Jesus Christ is the DOOR.**

Now we go back to the beginning, when Adam and Eve were given to dominate and rule this entire planet earth, but because they believed Satan's lies, as we still do to this very day, and they rejected their Living Creator God, Satan replaced their Creator God, and Satan became their god and ruler over them, and over their descendants. And to this very day, Satan is still the god of this age, as written in 2Corinthians 4:4, whose minds the god of this age has blinded, who do not believe.

142

Genesis 1:26 Then God said, "Let Us make man in Our image, according to Our likeness; let them have dominion over the fish of the sea, over the birds of the air, and over the cattle, over all the earth and over every creeping thing that creeps on the earth."

The present entire world is under Satan, and the entire world is following and worshipping Satan, and not knowing it. Nobody knows the Truth, and is not inclined to look for the **TRUTH, WHICH IS THE TRUE JESUS CHRIST. People are worshipping the creation, not the Living Creator God.**

We find written in Genesis 6:3 And the LORD said, "My Spirit shall not strive with man forever, for he is indeed flesh; yet his days shall be one hundred and twenty years." The word **years** in the original is written as שָׁנֶהשָׁנֶה**shâneh   shânâh,shaw-neh', shaw-naw'**

And it means a revolution of time, which can also refer to jubilee periods, a concept that is more applicable. A jubilee is a period of 49 years, as written in Leviticus 25:8 'And you shall count seven Sabbaths of years for yourself, seven times seven years; and the time of the seven Sabbaths of years shall be to you forty-nine years.

Leviticus 25:9 Then you shall cause the trumpet of the Jubilee to sound on the tenth day of the seventh month; on the Day of Atonement, you shall make the trumpet sound throughout all your land.

Leviticus 25:10 And you shall consecrate the fiftieth year, and proclaim liberty throughout all the land to all its inhabitants. It shall be a Jubilee for you; and each of you shall return to his possession, and each of you shall return to his family.

Leviticus 25:11 That fiftieth year shall be a Jubilee to you; in it you shall neither sow nor reap what grows of its own accord, nor gather the grapes of your untended vine.

Leviticus 25:12 For it is the Jubilee; it shall be holy to you; you shall eat its produce from the field.

The Jubilees will be observed and kept when Jesus Christ rules this planet during the one thousand years. Humanity will be happy to observe all the laws of God, as they are written in the books of the Bible, also known as the Word of God.

In this case of Jubilee times, it means that we are in the last Jubilee time period, or time cycle, of the six thousand years from Adam, which is the 120th jubilee, as discovered by Joseph Dumond at Sightedmoon.com

Sabbath	6th Cycle	5th Cycle	4th Cycle	3rd Cycle	2nd Cycle	1st Cycle
2044	2037	2030	2023	2016	2009	2002
2043	2036	2029	2022	2015	2008	2001
2042	2035	2028	2021	2014	2007	2000
2041	2034	2027	2020	2013	2006	1999
2040	2033	2026	2019	2012	2005	1998
2039	2032	2025	2018	2011	2004	1997
2038	2031	2024	2017	2010	2003	1996

This is part of the calendar published by Joseph Dumond, which I thoroughly checked and verified to be accurate and true. And this is the perfect time we are living in.

This is the 120th Jubilee Cycle, the last cycle under Satan's kingdom, just before Satan is locked away for a thousand years.

144

Jesus Christ said that Satan's time is going to be cut short. Satan will not be allowed to rule this planet until the end of the year 2044 A.D., which is the last year of this present 120th Jubilee Cycle. Satan's ruling time will be cut short, from between this time now and the end of 2044 A.D., as written in Matthew 24:22 . And unless those days were shortened, no flesh would be saved; (ALIVE) but for the elect's sake, those days will be shortened.

We are living in the 120 Jubilee Cycle. One cycle is 49 years. 120 cycles means we are living at the end of 5880 years from the creation of Adam.

In the book of Revelation, as we have already read, Satan is going to be locked up for one thousand years. The Living Creator God is a just God, and when Jesus Christ returns, He takes away time from Satan. After the one thousand years are up, Satan is let loose out of prison and is given back the time he missed out on. God has it all planned out, for a reason, and I will explain this to you, which you may have never heard of before.

When Satan is set loose, he starts to deceive mankind again, as I will explain later in this article, and as it is written in Revelation 20:7 Now when the thousand years have expired, Satan will be released from his prison Revelation 20:8 and will go out to deceive the nations which are in the four corners of the earth.

A resurrection brings back people to life again, from their restful death. They resurrect with a new body. There are two types of resurrections: one with a natural body, made of flesh and blood,

145

and another with a spirit body. Shortly, I will explain the difference between these two types of resurrections. Several resurrections are going to take place at various times, with different results, as written in 1 Corinthians 15:3. For I delivered to you first of all that which I also received: that Christ died for our sins according to the Scriptures.

1 Corinthians 15:4 and that He was buried, and that He rose again the third day according to the Scriptures. Jesus Christ was the first one to be resurrected immortal with a spirit body, after He was buried for three days and three nights.

1 Corinthians 15:22 For as in Adam all die, even so in Christ all shall be made alive.

1 Corinthians 15:23 But each one in his own order: Christ the first fruits, afterward those who are Christ's at His coming.

Jesus Christ was resurrected with a spiritual, immortal body. This is one type of resurrection. The saints are resurrected with the same resurrection that Jesus Christ experienced, having a spiritual, immortal body and eternal life. We know that the saints will resurrect with the same resurrection of Jesus Christ, with a spiritual body like Him, as written in 1 John 3:1 Behold what manner of love the Father has bestowed on us, that we should be called children of God! Therefore, the world does not know us, because it did not know Him.

1 John 3:2 Beloved, now we are children of God; and it has not yet been revealed what we shall be, but we know that when He is revealed, **we shall be like Him**, for we shall see Him as He

is.

The rest of mankind will be resurrected with a natural body, of flesh and blood, like the body they had before they died.

With a Spirit body, Jesus Christ could go through walls and closed doors, as written in John 20:19 Then, the same day at evening, being the first day of the week, when the doors were shut, where the disciples were assembled, for fear of the Jews, Jesus came and stood in the midst, and said to them, "Peace be with you."

Immediately after the resurrection of Jesus Christ, some of the Saints, who died before that time, were resurrected, AND AS SAINTS, THEY RESURRECTED WITH A SPIRIT BODY, and not to die again, the second death, and these saints were taken to Heaven, when Jesus Christ went to Heaven to present Himself to His Father, and also to present these few saints, who represent and are symbolized by the wave sheaf of the barley, that was waved at the Temple at 9:00 A M, on that Sunday morning, after Jesus Christ had risen, on Saturday sunset, as written in Matthew 27:52 , and the graves were opened; and many bodies of the saints who had fallen asleep were raised.

These were the very first handful of humans to go to Heaven, and they are called Elders. We have a written record of these saints, at the Throne of God in Heaven, as written in Revelation 11:16 . And the twenty-four elders who sat before God on their thrones fell on their faces and worshiped God.

Nobody was allowed to touch Jesus Christ, before He went

147

to Heaven, to present Himself and the resurrected saints to His Father, and we know this because it is written, in John 20:17 Jesus said to her, "Do not cling to Me, for I have not yet ascended to My Father; but go to My brethren and say to them, 'I am ascending to My Father and your Father, and to My God and your God.'"

Afterwards, Jesus Christ could be touched by many, as written in John 20:26. And after eight days, His disciples were again inside, and Thomas was with them. Jesus came, the doors being shut, and stood in the midst, and said, "Peace to you!"

John 20:27 Then He said to Thomas, "Reach your finger here, and look at My hands; and reach your hand here, and put it into My side. Do not be unbelieving, but believing."

John 20:28 And Thomas answered and said to Him, "My Lord and my God!"

These 24 Saints, who were resurrected at the same time as the resurrection of Jesus Christ has already received their Kingly Crowns. These saints are waiting in Heaven, to come down back to earth with Jesus Christ, when He returns, and these 24 Elders, will be given rule over cities in the Kingdom of God on this earth, as written in 1Thessolonians 4:14 For if we believe that Jesus died and rose again, even so God will bring with Him those who sleep in Jesus.

Luke 19:17 And he said to him, 'Well done, good servant; because you were faithful in a very little, have authority over ten cities.' Luke 19:18 And the second came, saying, 'Master, your mina has earned five minas. Luke 19:19 Likewise, he said to him, 'You also be over five cities.

When Jesus Christ returns to replace Satan and rule this planet, the saints will be Kings, ruling cities under Jesus Christ. They will have Gold crowns on their heads. Revelation 4:4 . Around the throne were twenty-four thrones, and on the thrones I saw twenty-four elders sitting, clothed in white robes; and they had crowns of gold on their heads.

The 24 Elders, who are in Heaven, removed their crowns, in honor of the One on the Throne in Heaven. As written in Revelation 4:10, the twenty-four elders fall down before Him who sits on the throne and worship Him who lives forever and ever, and cast their crowns before the throne, saying:

There are several different resurrections at different times, as the Apostle Paul wrote in 1Corinthians 15:20. But now Christ is risen from the dead, and has become the first fruits of those who have fallen asleep. There was no resurrection before this resurrection of Jesus Christ. 1Corinthians 15:21 For since by man came death, by Man also came the resurrection of the dead.

1 Corinthians 15:22 For as in Adam all die, even so in Christ all shall be made alive.

1 Corinthians 15:23 But **each one in his own order**: Christ the first fruits, afterward those who are Christ's at His coming.

Then we have another resurrection in the near future, of

the two of the Living Creator God's two end time Prophets, who will be preparing for Jesus Christ's return, and these two individuals, are going to stop the rain over this entire planet, for a period of three and a half years, while they will be fulfilling their mission, to get the attention of the people, because people will not want to hear their messages. We find this written in Revelation 11:3 And I will give power to my two witnesses, and they will prophesy one thousand two hundred and sixty days, clothed in sackcloth."

Revelation 11:4 These are the two olive trees and the two lamp stands standing before the God of the earth.

Revelation 11:5 And if anyone wants to harm them, fire proceeds from their mouth and devours their enemies. And if anyone wants to harm them, he must be killed in this manner.

Revelation 11:6 These have power to shut heaven, so that **no rain falls in the days of their prophecy**; and they have power over waters to turn them to blood, and to strike the earth with all plagues, as often as they desire.

Revelation 11:7 When they finish their testimony, the beast that ascends out of the bottomless pit will make war against them, overcome them, and kill them.

Revelation 11:8 And their dead bodies will lie in the street of the great city which spiritually is called Sodom and Egypt, where also our Lord was crucified.

Revelation 11:9 Then those from the peoples, tribes,

tongues, and nations will see their dead bodies three-and-a-half days, and not allow their dead bodies to be put into graves.

Revelation 11:10 And those who dwell on the earth will rejoice over them, make merry, and send gifts to one another, because these two prophets tormented those who dwell on the earth.

Revelation 11:11 Now after the three-and-a-half days, the breath of life from God entered them, and they stood on their feet, and great fear fell on those who saw them.

Revelation 11:12 And they heard a loud voice from heaven saying to them, "Come up here." And they ascended to heaven in a cloud, and their enemies saw them. These two will be the next to be resurrected from the dead and go to Heaven to receive their crown.

The Apostle Paul wrote about these imperishable Crowns from Heaven, as written in 1Corinthians 9:24 Do you not know that those who run in a race all run, but one receives the prize? Run in such a way that you may obtain it.

1 Corinthians 9:25 And everyone who competes for the prize is temperate in all things. Now they do it to obtain a perishable crown, but we for an imperishable crown.

2 Timothy 4:8 Finally, there is laid up for me the crown of righteousness, which the Lord, the righteous Judge, will give to me on that Day, and not to me only but also to all who have loved His appearing. This is the time of Jesus Christ appearing,

coming down from Heaven.

Revelation 3:11 Behold, I am coming quickly! Hold fast what you have, that no one may take your crown.

Now we have another Resurrection of the saints, in a few more years, on a Holy Feast Day of Pentecost, as written in 1 Thessalonians 4:16: 'For the Lord Himself will descend from heaven with a shout, with the voice of an archangel, and with the trumpet of God.' And the dead in Christ will rise first. 1 Thessalonians 4:17 Then we who are alive and remain shall be caught up together with them in the clouds, to meet the Lord in the air. And thus we shall always be with the Lord.

This verse shows that the saints who are alive, don't wait for Jesus Christ to touch land, but to meet Him in the air, and Jesus Christ will take them to Heaven to present them to His Father in Heaven, before they return back to this earth, a few months later, together with Jesus Christ. 1 Corinthians 15:50 Now this I say, brethren, that flesh and blood cannot inherit the kingdom of God; nor does corruption inherit incorruption. 1 Corinthians 15:51 Behold, I tell you a mystery: We shall not all sleep, but we shall all be changed— 1 Corinthians 15:52 in a moment, in the twinkling of an eye, at the last trumpet. For the trumpet will sound, and the dead will be raised incorruptible, and we shall be changed. 1 Corinthians 15:53 For this corruptible must put on incorruption, and this mortal must put on immortality.

Here we can see that Immortal life is given at this resurrection.

Jesus Christ will return back to Heaven, taking these saints with Him to present them to His Father in Heaven. We have a forerunner of this event taking place when, during the Annual Holy Feast Day of the Living Creator God, the Feast of Pentecost. At 9:00 AM, on this Annual Holy Feast Day of the Living Creator God, two loaves are waved to heaven, offering these two loaves to God the Father in Heaven, as written in Leviticus 23:17 You shall bring from your dwellings two wave loaves of two-tenths of an ephah. They shall be of fine flour; they shall be baked with leaven. They are the first fruits to the LORD.

These two loaves represent a batch of human beings, as first fruit, of becoming sons and daughters of the Living Creator God, from the rest of mankind. The offering of these saints in the near future, on the Annual Holy Feast Day called Pentecost, at 9:00 A.M. Jerusalem time, Jesus Christ will take the saints to Heaven to offer them to His Father, as the two loaves are offered to God on that Annual Holy Feast Day, of Pentecost.

Jesus Christ will bring all the saints from Heaven with Him when He returns back to earth, a few months later on the Annual Holy Feast Day of Trumpets, as written in 1 Thessalonians 4:14 For if we believe that Jesus died and rose again, even so God will bring with Him those who sleep in Jesus.

These saints will be kings and rulers in the Kingdom of God, the Government of God, with Jesus Christ on this earth, as written in Revelation 20:4 And I saw thrones, and they sat on them, and judgment was committed to them. Then I saw the souls of those who had been beheaded for their witness to Jesus and for the word of God, who had not worshiped the beast or his image, and had not received his mark on their foreheads or on their hands. And they lived and reigned with Christ for a thousand years.

This resurrection of the saints, which takes place on the Annual Holy Feast Day of Pentecost, these saints are represented with the wave of the first fruits Wheat, as written in Leviticus 23:15 'And you shall count for yourselves from the day after the Sabbath, from the day that you brought the sheaf of the wave offering: seven Sabbaths shall be completed.'

Leviticus 23:16 Count fifty days to the day after the seventh Sabbath; then you shall offer a new grain offering to the LORD.

On this resurrection from the dead, only the saints are resurrected; the rest of the dead will be resurrected at another time in the future, after the one thousand years are finished, as written in Revelation 20:5 But the rest of the dead did not live again until the thousand years were finished.

These two loves, one loaf represents the resurrected saints, and the other loaf represents the saints that are alive, when Jesus Christ comes down from Heaven, to take them to Heaven to present them to His Father.

God's Annual Festivals are based and formatted on The Living Creator God's Own Yearly Calendar, and they reveal the Living Creator God's plan for all mankind. God has all mankind in his plan, and does not want any human to perish, as it is written in 2Peter 3:9 . The Lord is not slack concerning His promise, as some count slackness, but is long-suffering toward us, not willing that any should perish but that all should come to repentance.

We know the year when Jesus Christ was born from historical records as written in Luke 2:1 . And it came to pass in those days that a decree went out from Caesar Augustus that all the world should be registered. Luke 2:2 This census first took place while Quirinius was governing Syria.

Jesus Christ was born on God's annual Holy Feast Day, called the Feast of Trumpets. It was the year 4 B.C. The month was September; it was at the New Moon, when the Crescent Moon appeared in the Western Horizon of Jerusalem. The New Moon declared the start of the Seventh Month, and the start of the annual Holy Feast Day, called the Feast of Trumpets. The time, as calculated by Astronomy was 7:40 PM, in Jerusalem, when the crescent Moon was visible, which declared the start of the Holy Feast Day of Trumpets, and Jesus Christ was born, at exactly that time, while Joseph was holding Mary's hand while the birth of Jesus Christ was taking place under the light from an oil lamp, that was inside a hole in the wall of the stable. Trumpets were heard from the clouds, with the angels singing songs of a newborn King.

Luke 2:13 And suddenly there was with the angel a multitude of the heavenly host praising God and saying: Luke 2:14 "Glory to God in the highest, And on earth peace, goodwill toward men!"

Trumpets are blown on the coronation of Kings, and when a King appears on the balcony to address the people. The King of Kings is going to appear, coming down from Heaven to lock up Satan and the demons, and to establish the Kingdom of God on this earth. The saints will be coming down from Heaven, with golden crowns on their heads. Trumpets will announce the approach of Jesus Christ as King, together with His saints, also as Kings. Revelation 19:16 And He has on His robe and on His thigh a name written: **KING OF KINGS** AND LORD OF LORDS. Revelation 1:7 Behold, He is coming with clouds, and **every eye will see Him**, even they who pierced Him. And all the tribes of the earth will mourn because of Him. Even so, Amen.

He will appear coming down from Heaven after sunset, after the new crescent moon appears on the western horizon of Jerusalem, declaring the start of the Seventh Month - the Holy Feast Day of Trumpets. People are asleep, and that day will come on them unawares, as a thief in the night.

THE REAPER IS COMING AT NIGHT - WHILE EVERYONE IS ASLEEP

1Thessalonians 5:2 For you yourselves know perfectly that the day of the Lord so comes as a thief in the night.

Matthew 25:26 "But his Lord answered and said to him, 'You wicked and lazy servant, **you knew that I reap where I have not sown,**

Revelation 14:14 Then I looked, and behold, a white cloud, and on the cloud sat One like the **Son of Man**, having on His head a golden crown, and in His hand a sharp sickle. Revelation 14:15 And another angel came out of the temple, crying with a loud voice to Him who sat on the cloud, "Thrust in Your sickle and reap, for the time has come for You to reap, for the harvest of the earth is ripe." Revelation 14:16 So He who sat on the cloud thrust in His sickle on the earth, **and the earth was reaped.**

God's annual Holy Feast Day, called the Feast of Trumpets, is celebrated with great shouts of joy, because it is **Jesus Christ's Birthday celebration**, as written in Psalms 98:4 : Shout joyfully to the LORD, all the earth; Break forth in song, rejoice, and sing praises. Psalms 98:5 Sing to the LORD with the harp, With the harp and the sound of a psalm. Psalms 98:6 **With trumpets** and the sound of a horn; **Shout joyfully before the LORD, the King.** Psalms 98:7 Let the sea roar, and all its fullness, The world and those who dwell in it; Psalms 98:8 Let the rivers clap their hands; Let the hills be joyful together before the LORD.

Psalms 98:9 **For He is coming to judge the earth.** With righteousness He shall judge the world, And the peoples with equity.

Every eye will see Jesus Christ coming down from Heaven.

On that day, the saints will be kings forever, in the Kingdom of God on this earth.

Jesus Christ was born on that Annual Holy Feast Day of Trumpets, and it is expected that Jesus Christ will also return with His saints from Heaven, on that same Annual Holy Feast Day of Trumpets. Leviticus 23:23 Then the LORD spoke to Moses, saying, Leviticus 23:24 "Speak to the children of Israel, saying:

'In the seventh month, on the first day of the month, you shall have a Sabbath-rest, a memorial of blowing of trumpets, a holy convocation. Leviticus 23:25 You shall do no customary work on it; and you shall offer an offering made by fire to the LORD.' "

Jesus Christ said that nobody will know the day or the hour, not even Himself, because His Father in Heaven will decide the day and the hour. The year is set already, and does not change, and it can be known by the faithful ones, the saints who are alive, who are keeping and living by all the commandments of God. Jesus Christ didn't say that nobody will know the year, but only the day and the hour, as written in Matthew 24:36: "But of that day and hour no one knows, not even the angels of heaven, but My Father only.

The Holy Feast Day of Trumpets starts when the CRESCENT NEW MOON signals the start of the seventh month of The Living Creator God Calendar, and it is seen and witnessed by two witnesses in Jerusalem. God the Father decides and controls the sighting of the **CRESCENT NEW MOON, and it is His decision on the spot,** if the sixth month ends with 29 days or is delayed by one day, ending the sixth month with 30 days. This is why Jesus Christ said, as written in Matthew 24:36, "But of that day and hour no one knows, not even the angels of heaven, but My Father only.

The Elect, those belonging to the Living Creator God, that day will not come on them as a snare or a surprise. They will be watching and waiting for that day as written in, 1Thessalonians

5:4 But you, brethren, are not in darkness, so that this Day should overtake you as a thief. 1Thessalonians 5:5 You are all sons of light and sons of the day. We are not of the night nor of darkness. 1Thessalonians 5:6 Therefore let us not sleep, as others do, but let us watch and be sober.

Nobody will be entered into the kingdom of the Living Creator God without keeping those ten commandments; it is an absolute requirement, and without window climbing, or entering from other back doors. Only Jesus Christ is the door, as written in John 10:7 . Then Jesus said to them again, "Most assuredly, I say to you, I am the door of the sheep. John 10:9 I am the door. If anyone enters by Me, he will be saved, and will go in and out and find pasture. John 10:1 "Most assuredly, I say to you, he who does not enter the sheepfold by the door, but climbs up some other way, the same is a thief and a robber. And thieves and robbers will not enter the Kingdom of God or become a son or daughter of God, as written in Revelation 21:7 . He who overcomes shall inherit all things, and I will be his God and he shall be My son. Revelation 21:8 But the cowardly, unbelieving, abominable, murderers, sexually immoral, sorcerers, idolaters, and all liars shall have their part in the lake which burns with fire and brimstone, which is **the second death." To have a second death means that the individual has lived two life spans.**

The second death by fire means to be turned into ashes, not burning alive forever.

This verse confirms that there are two life spans that

people will experience, and very few may choose to die a second time, a second death, by being burned out and reduced to ashes, never to live again. And that means not only their physical body, but also the real entity, which is the soul, using that physical body. where it says that God has the power to destroy both soul and physical bodies, as written in Matthew 10:28 And do not fear those who kill the body but cannot kill the soul. But rather fear Him who is **able to destroy both soul and body**. Something destroyed is put out of existence.

To have an immortal life, the key is to keep the Ten Commandments. When the Kingdom of God is established, here on this planet, at the return of Jesus Christ, this whole planet will be governed by the Ten Commandments as written in Matthew 19:16 . Now behold, one came and said to Him, "Good Teacher, what good thing shall I do that I may have eternal life?" Matthew 19:17 So He said to him, "Why do you call Me good? No one is good but One, that is, God. But if you want to enter into life, keep the commandments."

Matthew 19:18 He said to Him, "Which ones?" Jesus said, " 'YOU SHALL NOT MURDER,' 'YOU SHALL NOT COMMIT ADULTERY,' 'YOU SHALL NOT STEAL,' 'YOU SHALL NOT BEAR FALSE WITNESS,' Matthew 19:19 'HONOR YOUR FATHER AND YOUR MOTHER,' and 'YOU SHALL LOVE YOUR NEIGHBOR AS YOURSELF.' "

The Apostle Paul made it very clear that the timing of the seasons for the return of Jesus Christ will be revealed, as written in 1 Thessalonians, as I have written earlier.

The Apostle Paul says that those who are following and keeping the real and true, God's Calendar, and keeping God's Annual Holy Feast Days, at the right times, will not be left in the dark, and they will know the Season when Jesus Christ will return.

1Thessalonians 5:1 But concerning the times and the seasons, brethren, you have no need that I should write to you.

1Thessalonians 5:2 For you yourselves know perfectly that the day of the Lord so comes as a thief in the night.

1Thessalonians 5:3 For when they say, "Peace and safety!" then sudden destruction comes upon them, as labor pains upon a pregnant woman. And they shall not escape.

All this means that the living saints, who are living by the Laws of God, will know the season time of the return of Jesus Christ, but it will be like a thief in the night, for the rest of mankind. It will be a day when they are not waiting for it.

Here, Paul mentions the season. This can refer to the crescent moon of the seventh month, pronouncing the Annual Holy Feast Day of Trumpets. The moon was created to show the seasons, as written in Genesis 1:14 . Then God said, "Let there be lights in the firmament of the heavens to divide the day from the night; and let them be for signs and seasons, and for days and years;

The Living Creator God's Calendar is under the control of God the Father. He chooses when to start His New Year and when to set the timing of when His annual Holy Feast days are to be kept. The start of every year of the Living Creator God's Calendar, starts by having enough barley for the wave sheaf offering, during the Feast of Unleavened Bread, as written in Leviticus 23:9 And the LORD spoke to Moses, saying, Leviticus 23:10 "Speak to the children of Israel, and say to them: 'When you come into the land which I give to you, and reap its harvest, then you shall bring a sheaf of the first fruits of your harvest to the priest.

Leviticus 23:11 He shall wave the sheaf before the LORD, to be accepted on your behalf; on the day after the Sabbath, the priest shall wave it.

This was the correct and true system kept, and as followed by Jesus Christ Himself, and sure enough, Jesus Christ kept His Father's annual holy Feast Days at the right times. I hope that this makes it very clear to the reader of this article, that to start God's Calendar Year, by any other method, at any other different times, will end up keeping the Living Creator God's Annual Holy Feast Days, at the wrong times of the year, and making - changing God's Feasts, and making them your own Feasts, by dictating to the Living Creator God by your decisions, and by setting your own timing, when to have your Annual Feasts. You will be making and creating Holy Time, that which is not Holy, making yourself more righteous than your Living Creator God.

If we follow the footsteps of Jesus Christ, of how He kept His Father's Calendar, we cannot go wrong, and we will be keeping The Holy annual Feasts at the right times, the same as

Jesus Christ did. And this is the correct way.

It is the Living Creator God who sets up the appointment times, of when you are to appear before Him, three times during the year, as written in Exodus 23:14 "Three times you shall keep a feast to Me in the year: Exodus 23:15 You shall keep the Feast of Unleavened Bread (you shall eat unleavened bread seven days, as I commanded you, at the time appointed in the month of Abib, for in it you came out of Egypt; none shall appear before Me empty);

Exodus 23:17 "Three times in the year all your males shall appear before the Lord GOD.

If you decide to start God's Calendar, any other way, and by doing so, you set up your own timings, of when to go and appear before your God, by making your own appointment times, the Living Creator.

The Living Creator God says to you the following, as written in Isaiah 1:12 : "When you come to appear before Me, Who has required this from your hand, To trample My courts?

In other words, you appeared before your Living Creator God at a time when you were not invited, and you trampled God's Heaven.

Your God continues on to tell you not to go to him, He does not want to see you, and He hates your set Feasts, He does not want to hear your prayers, He cover His eyes, because He does not want to see you, as written in Isaiah 1:13 Bring no more futile sacrifices; Incense is an abomination to Me. The New Moons, the Sabbaths, and the calling of assemblies—I cannot endure iniquity and the sacred meeting.

Isaiah 1:14 Your New Moons and your appointed feasts My soul hates; They are a trouble to Me, I am weary of bearing them.

The new moons mentioned here are the start of the moon months, not according to God's way.

Isaiah 1:15 When you spread out your hands, I will hide My eyes from you; Even though you make many prayers, I will not hear. Your hands are full of blood.

I hope that I have made it clear enough for you that this is a very serious matter, of when to appear before your God, three times a year, on the appointed times, when God invites you, and the times that He wants you to appear before Him. If you choose your own times to go and meet Him, He will not be there for you, and you will not find Him.

Also, during the time when Jesus Christ lived in Jerusalem, the lunar months started when the first crescent moon was visible, and witnessed by two people. We have a written record of this by the Jewish historian Philo, who lived at the same time as Jesus Christ.

If Jesus Christ recognized and observed the New Moons, as recorded by Philo, the same system is to be followed today, as it was the way Jesus Christ started the New Moons. Jesus Christ is the same yesterday, today, and forever, with no changes. **What Jesus Christ lived by and observed when He lived in Jerusalem is the same today and forever.** Hebrews 13:8 Jesus Christ is the same yesterday, today, and forever.

In other words, we are to start the New Moons with the same system as Jesus Christ practiced when He was alive. Jesus Christ set examples for us to follow, and not to be confused by Satan's way of life.

If you start the moon month by a calculation method, and you don't see the crescent moon in the sky, you lie to yourself, and if, within that moon month, there is an Annual Holy Feast day, you will be keeping the Holy Feast Day on the wrong day.

Philo was a prominent Jewish leader who lived in Alexandria from about 20 B.C.E. to about 50 A.D. He lived during the same time as Jesus Christ. Philo was a contemporary of both Jesus Christ and the Apostle Paul. He was aware of what Jesus Christ and His followers considered was the new moon, as the start of a New Month on God's Calendar. In his Treatise on the Special Laws, Philo **discusses the Biblical observances.** Note how he describes the new moon: "[It] is that which comes after the conjunction, which… [is] the day of the new moon in each month."

In his detailed discussion of the new moon, Philo describes what constitutes a new moon: "…**at the time of the new moon, the sun begins to illuminate the moon with a light which** is visible to the outward senses, [eyesight] and then she [the Moon] displays her own beauty to the beholders."

As Philo noted, the new moon follows the conjunction, but it is not the conjunction itself. His observation reveals to us what was considered the new moon in Jesus Christ's day, and what the Saviour Jesus Christ Himself also observed and followed as the new moon, as the start of a New Month. **That is all we need to know to realize what still constitutes the Biblical new moon today.**

If Jesus Christ observed the New Moons in any other way than the instituted set observation of the New crescent moon, as described by the historian Philo, He would have been stoned to death, well before the time of His crucifixion.

When studying Philo's records, it becomes clear how the New Moons were observed and when they began, at the time of Jesus Christ. Philo leaves us no question of how we are to be observing the New Moons today, with the sighted New Crescent Moons.

Then, when Jesus Christ returns, you go complaining to Him because you are still in a physical, flesh-and-blood body. You were not changed to an immortal body. Sad to say, the following answer you will receive from Jesus Christ, as written in Matthew 7:21: "Not everyone who says to Me, 'Lord, Lord,' shall enter the kingdom of heaven, but he who does the will of My Father in heaven.

167

Matthew 7:22 Many will say to Me in that day, 'Lord, Lord, have we not prophesied in Your name, cast out demons in Your name, and done many wonders in Your name?'

Matthew 7:23 And then I will declare to them, 'I never knew you; depart from Me, you who practice lawlessness!'

1John 3:4 Whoever commits sin also commits lawlessness, and sin is lawlessness.

It is the Barley which starts to ripen; at that time, it is to be waved. We wave to someone to say goodbye. In Malta to this very day, the barley is called **XEJR,** which translates into the English language as WAVES, like when waving to someone. In this ritual, the first of the ripened barley is waved to God the Father.

God the Father controls the weather, and He is able to control the growth and the ripening of the wild barley growing in Jerusalem with the rain and the temperature. And the first month on God's calendar is when the new crescent moon is seen from Jerusalem, provided with a handful of ripened barley, enough to perform the Wave Sheaf Offering. This first month of the moon sets out the timing of all God's annual Holy Feasts during the whole year.

Only enough ripened barley, for the Wave Sheaf Offering, is required to start the first moon of God's Calendar year. This is a handful of ripened first fruit barley, to be offered to God in Heaven, also representing the handful of the resurrected saints, who resurrected at the same time when Jesus Christ was resurrected, whom Jesus Christ took up to Heaven with Him, to offer them to His Father in Heaven, as I have written earlier, and as written in Matthew 27:52 and the graves were opened; and many bodies of the saints who had fallen asleep were raised;

Matthew 27:53 and coming out of the graves after His resurrection, they went into the holy city and appeared to many.

Also, the Apostle Paul mentions these saints, led by Jesus Christ, as written in Ephesians 4:8 . Therefore, He says: "WHEN HE ASCENDED ON HIGH, HE LED CAPTIVITY CAPTIVE, AND GAVE GIFTS TO MEN."

Ephesians 4:9 (Now this, "HE ASCENDED"—what does it mean but that He also first descended into the lower parts of the earth?

Ephesians 4:10 He who descended is also the One who ascended far above all the heavens, that He might fill all things.)

The entire world is living in the captivity of Satan. These saints were also captives of Satan, and by their resurrections became free, and were led by Jesus Christ, and received their gifts in Heaven. They were righteous men, and in Heaven, crowns were placed on their heads, as recorded in the Book of Revelation.

This handful of saints is still there in Heaven, and these saints are the 24 Elders mentioned in Revelation 4:4 . Around the throne were twenty-four thrones, and on the thrones I saw twenty-four elders sitting, clothed in white robes; and they had crowns of gold on their heads.

God the Father is in control of His Calendar, and does not leave it to anybody else to decide when to start the year. God the Father decides if the year ends with twelve moons, or if it ends with thirteen moons. This is the reason why the Feast of Trumpets is impossible to figure out ahead of time; God the Father is in control of it.

The Annual Holy Feast Day of Trumpets is on the first day of the seventh month on God's Calendar, as written in Leviticus 23:24 "Speak to the children of Israel, saying: 'In the seventh month, on the first day of the month, you shall have a Sabbath-rest, a memorial of blowing of trumpets, a holy

As written earlier, I like to remind you again, God the Father may decide to have the sixth month end with 29 days, letting the crescent moon be seen, after sunset of the 29th day, indicating the start of the first day of the seventh month with the Holy Feast Day of Trumpets.

Also, God the Father may, at the last minute, decide to have the sixth month end with a 30-day month by spreading a blanket of darkness, covering Jerusalem and hiding the new crescent moon from view. This makes it the sixth moon month to be a 30-day moon month, making the next day, after the 30th day, the first day of the seventh month. This marks the beginning of the Annual Holy Feast Day of Trumpets, the Holy Day on which Jesus Christ is expected to return one day.

Jesus Christ was born on the first day of the seventh month on God's Calendar, and that is the day when His birthday is celebrated with an annual Holy Feast day, called the Feast of Trumpets, as I mentioned earlier. The Trumpets are blown when a King appears. How much more are the trumpets to be blown when the King of Kings appears, coming down from Heaven, with thousands of other Kings with Him!

As Jesus Christ was born on this first day of the seventh month, He will also be appearing again, coming down from Heaven, on the same first day of this seventh month, which is a Holy Annual Feast day of Trumpets, as I have written earlier in this article. The Trumpets are blown to declare **THE COMING KING OF KINGS.**

Those living at that time, by not expecting the return of Jesus Christ, may be caught working on that Annual Holy Feast Day of Trumpets.

This seventh month cannot start until the new sighted crescent moon is sighted from Jerusalem, AND WITNESSED BY TWO WITNESSES. The sighting of this seventh moon month from Jerusalem is again under the control of God the Father, and He controls whether the moon can be sighted on the 29th day or the 30th day of the sixth month. The timing of sighting the crescent moon, which indicates the start of the first day of the seventh month, varies every month, and this is the reason why Jesus Christ said that nobody knows the day or the hour. Jesus Christ did not say that we will not know the year, and the month, as time progresses on, as written in Matthew 24:36: "But of that day and hour no one knows, not even the angels of heaven, but

My Father only.

This is because God the Father decides the day, right there on the spot, unexpected by everyone else.

When Jesus Christ is returning to this earth, with His saints and His Heavenly armies, every eye will see Him coming. As mentioned earlier, Jesus Christ will be fighting a battle with Satan and with Satan's armies in Armageddon, as written in Revelation 20:2 . He laid hold of the dragon, that serpent of old, who is the Devil and Satan, and bound him for a thousand years.

Satan will be judged and sentenced to be locked away for one thousand years, and during those one thousand years, the Kingdom of God will be governing this entire planet without the presence of Satan. People will be living by God's way of life, as it was intended from the very beginning of creation, at the time when Adam and Eve were created.

It was Satan who brought death and sufferings on all humans for these six thousand years. With Satan put away, his death and sufferings will be locked away with him, and under God's Kingdom, this earth will turn into an oasis, a restful, peaceful, and happy state. This will be the seventh millennium of creation. The soon coming one thousand years are represented by every weekly Sabbath, the seventh day of every week, which is a Holy Sabbath Day of rest. Those living during these one thousand years will be living a restful, healthy life.

Regarding this restful period of one thousand years, similar to the restful time of the weekly Sabbath, under Jesus

Christ, we have a reference to it as written in Hebrews 4:9 : There remains therefore a rest for the people of God.

Hebrews 4:10 For he who has entered His rest has himself also ceased from his works as God did from His.

Hebrews 4:11 Let us therefore be diligent to enter that rest, lest anyone fall according to the same example of disobedience.

These one thousand years, which are soon going to start, are also represented with the Sabbatical years of rest, when also the Land rests every seven years. People will be having a peaceful, easy life, without sickness, and without suffering, and with no more crying, as written in Leviticus 25:2: "Speak to the children of Israel, and say to them: 'When you come into the land which I give you, then the land shall keep a Sabbath to the LORD.

Leviticus 25:3 Six years you shall sow your field, and six years you shall prune your vineyard, and gather its fruit.

As the seventh day of the week is Holy and a day of rest. And as every seventh year is also a Sabbath year of rest for both the people and the land, as written in Leviticus 25:4 , but in the seventh year there shall be a Sabbath of solemn rest for the land, a Sabbath to the LORD. You shall neither sow your field nor prune your vineyard.

Leviticus 25:5 What grows of its own accord of your harvest you shall not reap, nor gather the grapes of your untended vine, for it is a year of rest for the land.

This shows us that also the seventh Millennium is going to be a thousand years of rest for those living during the one thousand years under the rule of Jesus Christ. Those living in the soon coming one thousand years, the land will be producing abundant free food for all humanity, as it is during the Sabbatical year. People will gather food freely six days a week, from what God provides, and rest on the Seventh, the weekly Holy Sabbath Day, in the same way that the Living Creator God gave Israel manna six days a week.

As I wrote earlier, God prepared a garden to feed mankind before creating Adam and Eve. Maybe God will be feeding humanity during the coming one thousand years. And people will be relaxing everyone under their fig tree as written in Micah 4:4 . But everyone shall sit under his vine and under his fig tree, And no one shall make them afraid; For the mouth of the LORD of hosts has spoken.

Singing and happiness will abound during these one thousand years. Isaiah 35:4 Say to those who are fearful-hearted, "Be strong, do not fear! Behold, your God will come with vengeance, With the recompense of God; He will come and save you."

Isaiah 35:5 Then the eyes of the blind shall be opened, And the ears of the deaf shall be unstopped. Isaiah 35:6 Then the lame shall leap like a deer, And the tongue of the dumb sing. For waters shall burst forth in the wilderness, And streams in the desert.

Will those lame, who had a limb amputated, have their limb grow back and be able to leap and dance? Everything is possible with the Living Creator God. Matthew 19:26 But Jesus looked at them and said to them, "With men this is impossible, but **with God all things are possible."** Jeremiah 31:13 "Then shall the virgin rejoice in the dance, And the young men and the old, together; For I will turn their mourning to joy, Will comfort them, And make them rejoice rather than sorrow.

Isaiah 35:7 The parched ground shall become a pool, And the thirsty land springs of water; In the habitation of jackals, where each lay, There shall be grass with reeds and rushes.

Isaiah 11:5 Righteousness shall be the belt of His loins, And faithfulness the belt of His waist.

Isaiah 11:6 "The wolf also shall dwell with the lamb, The leopard shall lie down with the young goat, The calf and the young lion and the fatling together; And a little child shall lead them."

Isaiah 11:7 The cow and the bear shall graze; Their young ones shall lie down together; And the lion shall eat straw like the ox.

Isaiah 11:8 The nursing child shall play by the cobra's hole, And the weaned child shall put his hand in the viper's den.

Isaiah 11:9 They shall not hurt nor destroy in all My holy mountain, For the earth shall be full of the knowledge of the LORD As the waters cover the sea.

During the next one thousand years, starting very soon,

everyone on earth will learn about the True Living Creator God. Those still living, who will enter the next one thousand years, will forget Satan, and the hard way of life, of lies, sorrow, and deceit, and how they lived with Satanic traditions, and will learn to live God's way of life. And all those who are born in the next one thousand years, will be living under the kingdom of God, in safety, without fear of wars, as written in Micah 4:2 Many nations shall come and say, "Come, and let us go up to the mountain of the LORD, To the house of the God of Jacob; He will teach us His ways, And we shall walk in His paths." For out of Zion the law shall go forth, And the word of the LORD from Jerusalem.

Micah 4:3 He shall judge between many peoples, And rebuke strong nations afar off; They shall beat their swords into plowshares, And their spears into pruning hooks; Nation shall not lift up sword against nation, Neither shall they learn war anymore.

In the next thousand years, under the rule of Jesus Christ, people will want to follow and live the way of life that the Living Creator God has ordained. They will only have one way of Life, which will be different from the one we are living in today, with many different traditions, under and controlled by Satan's lies and beliefs. People will live under the Kingdom of God, in the truth, and not in lies. It will be a different life, compared to the one that was under Satan's government. People will be living in peace for one thousand years, as written in Isaiah 2:3. Many people shall come and say, "Come, and let us go up to the mountain of the

176

LORD, To the house of the God of Jacob; He will teach us His ways, And we shall walk in His paths." For out of Zion shall go forth the law, And the word of the LORD from Jerusalem.

Isaiah 2:4 He shall judge between the nations, And rebuke many people; They shall beat their swords into plowshares, And their spears into pruning hooks; Nation shall not lift up sword against nation, Neither shall they learn war anymore.

This is a one thousand years of rest, in the same way as when the Living Creator God, rested from His work, on the seventh day of creation week as written in Genesis 2:2 And on the seventh day God ended His work which He had done, and He rested on the seventh day from all His work which He had done.

People will make a change, and so will the animals, when Jesus Christ starts to rule this earth, with the Kingdom of God, as written earlier. The lions will start eating grass, instead of hunting for meat. They will change over to vegetarians as written in Isaiah 65:25 The wolf and the lamb shall feed together, The lion shall eat straw like the ox, And dust shall be the serpent's food. They shall not hurt nor destroy in all My holy mountain," Says the LORD.

At the close of the one thousand years, Satan is let out of prison, as written in Revelation 20:7. Now, when the thousand years have expired, Satan will be released from his prison.

Now all these people, who lived for one thousand years of rest, and in peace and harmony, are going to taste and experience Satan's way of life, as we are at present going through under Satan.

Now the Living Creator God is going to give Satan the same number of years that the Living Creator God took away from Satan to save this planet, as I wrote earlier. With Satan let loose, these people living at that time will live and experience both ways of life: life under God's Kingdom and life under Satan for a few years. Now they can make a choice, because now they have experienced both ways of life. They will either choose eternal death under Satan's way of life, or eternal life in the Kingdom of God, as children in the Family of the Living Creator God, and live forever with the Living Creator God.

When Satan is let out of prison, he is going to make wars between the nations, as he is doing now at our time, as written in Revelation 20:7. Now, when the thousand years have expired, Satan will be released from his prison. Revelation 20:8 and will go out to deceive the nations which are in the four corners of the earth, Gog and Magog, to gather them together to battle, whose number is as the sand of the sea. Revelation 20:9 They went up on the breadth of the earth and surrounded the camp of the saints and the beloved city. And fire came down from God out of heaven and devoured them.

Those who were devoured died their first death and will await their resurrection to receive their second death by fire. They will die their **SECOND DEATH AGAIN BY FIRE,** as I will explain later on.

From here on, the Living Creator God, does not need to have Satan around anymore, and the Living Creator God will destroy Satan, and his demons by a prepared fire that comes down from Heaven, as written in Revelation 20:10 The devil, who deceived them, was cast into the lake of fire and brimstone where the beast and the false prophet were cast. Matthew 25:41 "Then He will also say to those on the left hand, 'Depart from Me, you cursed, into the everlasting fire prepared for the devil and his angels. ' This Fire will make everything ashes.

Those who choose the Living Creator God at that time of the end of the coming one thousand years, will instantly, be changed into immortal, spirit beings, in a twinkling of an eye, in the same manner, as those saints, who were living and met Jesus Christ, in the air, as written earlier in 1 Corinthians 15:51 Behold, I tell you a mystery: We shall not all sleep, but we shall all be changed—1 Corinthians 15:52 in a moment, in the twinkling of an eye, at the last trumpet. For the trumpet will sound, and the dead will be raised incorruptible, and we shall be changed.

These will become part of the Living Creator God's Family forever, and they become first to be in God's Family, before those who lived under the first period of six thousand years rule under Satan, those who only have tasted and experienced Satan's way of life.

Jesus Christ said the following: - Matthew 20:8 "So when evening had come, the owner of the vineyard said to his steward, 'Call the laborers and give them their wages, beginning with the last to the first.' Notice that the last are going to receive their down payment before those who were first in the field. The first group of people, those who lived on this earth from the time of Adam to the time Jesus Christ returns, is the first group. The last group of people is those who are going to be born and live for one thousand years from the time that Jesus Christ returns to this earth to rule this earth with the Government of the Living Creator God. There will be no more births after the end of these one thousand years.

The wages mentioned here refer to receiving **ETERNAL LIFE**. Every human will receive the same wage, which is **ETERNAL LIFE.** The first group who lived under the burden of Satan for six thousand years complained, because they had a lifetime of hard life under the burden of Satan's rule, as written in Matthew 20:10 . But when the first came, they supposed that they would receive more; and they likewise received each a denarius. Matthew 20:11 And when they had received it, they complained against the landowner, Matthew 20:12 saying, 'These last men have worked only one hour, and you made them equal to us who have borne the burden and the heat of the day.'

This first group of people lived for six thousand years under Satan, and the last group of people is going to live for only a very few years under Satan, only the few years when Satan is let out of prison, for a very short time, after the one thousand years being locked away. Revelation 20:3But after these things he must be released for a little while.

Matthew 20:13 But he answered one of them and said, 'Friend, I am doing you no wrong. Did you not agree with me for a denarius? The Living Creator God promised that He would give us **ETERNAL LIFE**, and this is the denarius payment mentioned here.

John 4:35 Do you not say, 'There are still four months and then comes the harvest'? Behold, I say to you, lift up your eyes and look at the fields, for they are already white for harvest! John 4:36 And **he who reaps receives wages**, and **gathers fruit for ETERNAL LIFE,** that both he who sows and he who reaps may rejoice together.

It is very clear here what Jesus Christ is talking about: that the wages are **ETERNAL LIFE.**

Jesus Christ made it very clear that there are two groups of people living under different times, when He said, as written in Matthew 20:16 So the last will be first, and the first last. For many are called, but few are chosen." Those who are going to be living in the coming one thousand years will have access to receive **ETERNAL LIFE,** before the resurrection of all those who died from the time of Adam to the time of when Jesus Christ returns to rule this planet. Revelation 20:5 But the rest of the dead did not live again until the thousand years were finished. This is so important that this statement of Jesus Christ, saying, Matthew 20:16 So the last will be first, and the first last, " is also recorded in Mark 9 and Luke 13.

Jesus Christ said, The last come first, and the first come last, as written in Matthew 20:15 . Is it not lawful for me to do what I wish with my own things? Or is your eye evil because I am good?'

Luke 13:30 And indeed there are some that are last who will be first, and there are first who will be last."

You and I, if we die before Jesus Christ returns, we are included in this first lot of people living under Satan. If we are still alive when Jesus Christ returns, we will be counted with the last lot of people, and we will continue living for one thousand years under the Kingdom of God.

The last lot are all those who lived during the coming one thousand years, ruled by Jesus Christ, when Jesus Christ returns. Those Last ones are the ones who lived and were born during the one thousand years of Jesus Christ's rule, with the Kingdom of God, and are the last lot of humans to be born in that period of one thousand years. This also tells us that during the eight Millennium, there will be no more human births. When the first lot of people are resurrected, those who lived as captives under Satan. This first lot will live under the Kingdom of God for one thousand years, just as the last lot did.

The living Creator God is Fair, as it is written in Deuteronomy 10:17 For the LORD your God is God of gods and Lord of Lords, the great God, mighty and awesome, who shows no partiality nor takes a bribe. Acts 10:34 Then Peter opened his mouth and said: "In truth I perceive that God shows no partiality. Ephesians 6:9 And you, masters, do the same things to them, giving up threatening, knowing that your own Master also is in heaven, and there is no partiality with Him.

Therefore, as the next generation will live under the Living

182

Creator God's Government for one thousand years, those resurrected for the eighth Millennium will also live one thousand years under the Living Creator God's Kingdom.

Remember what I wrote earlier, that **ONE DAY**, to the Living Creator God, means ONE THOUSAND **YEARS.** Also, as I wrote earlier, Martha, Lazarus' sister, referred to this eighth millennium as the resurrection of the **LAST DAY. It also means the Last One Thousand Years in the Living Creator God's Plan for mankind.**

In the near future, at the start of the next thousand years, billions of babies will be born under the Kingdom of the Living Creator God. Now we must consider that babies are not yet able to make decisions. Here I ask the question: At what age does God expect humans to make the decisions of **LIFE OR DEATH?**

I will go to the time when Israel was in the wilderness, when the Living Creator God made a decision that only those under the age of twenty years were allowed to enter the promised land. And all those over the age of twenty years old, had to die in the wilderness, as written in Numbers 32:10 So the LORD's anger was aroused on that day, and He swore an oath, saying,

Numbers 32:11 'Surely none of the men who came up from Egypt, from twenty years old and above, shall see the land of which I swore to Abraham, Isaac, and Jacob, because they have not wholly followed Me.'

The Living Creator God regarded all those under the age of twenty years as innocent people, and regarded them as incapable of making decisions, and separated them from the rebels of those over twenty years old. This means that all those over twenty years old were capable of making decisions.

From these verses, we can determine the age at which the Living Creator God works. He chooses the age of those over the age of twenty years to make their individual decisions. From this, we come to the conclusion that twenty years before the end of the next one thousand years ruled by Jesus Christ, there will be no more births of human babies. The reason for this is that the last baby born will be twenty years old at the end of the one thousand years, when Satan is let loose from prison. And the last baby at twenty years old will be able to make a decision to either have **ETERNAL LIFE**, by choosing the Living Creator God's way of life, or receive **ETERNAL DEATH**, by choosing Satan's way of life.

If God is going to give one thousand years to the last lot of people, ruled by God's Kingdom, God, He is also going to give the first lot of people, after their resurrection from the dead, another one thousand years of life, ruled by the Kingdom of God, because God is not a respecter of persons, as written in Romans 2:11 For there is no partiality with God.

I am referring to one day for one thousand years, represented with the Eighth Day following the Feast of Tabernacles, as written in Leviticus 23:36 For seven days you shall offer an offering made by fire to the LORD. On the eighth day, you shall have a holy convocation, and you shall offer an

184

offering made by fire to the LORD. It is a sacred assembly, and you shall do no customary work on it.

From the Scripture, we know that the Living Creator God has planned eight thousand years to deal with His mankind.

Even Martha knew about this eight-day resurrection, when she expected to meet her brother Lazarus again with a resurrection, as written in John 11:24 . Martha said to Him, "I know that he will rise again in the resurrection at the last day."

Those who lived for a thousand years under Jesus Christ's Government, and some may unfortunately choose Satan, will die their first death, and wait for their resurrection to receive their **SECOND DEATH**, to be terminated forever, as I mentioned earlier, and I will explain in more detail a little later.

From here on, God does not need to have Satan around anymore, and God will destroy Satan and his demons. When Satan fulfills the time allotted to him, after he is released from prison, he and his demons will be destroyed forever, never to exist again, as written in Revelation 20:10 . The devil, who deceived them, was cast into the lake of fire and brimstone.

This is a different fire from the one we use for cooking. This is a prepared fire that comes down from Heaven. The Living Creator God has prepared this unique fire a long time ago as written in, Matthew 25:41 the everlasting fire prepared for the devil and his angels: It will be a fire that will destroy both soul and body, the one Jesus Christ mentioned in, Matthew 10:28 And do not fear those who kill the body but cannot kill the soul. But rather fear Him who is able to destroy both soul and body in hell.

Now we come to all those who lived and who died under Satan's first six thousand years' rule, from the time of Adam to the time of the return of Jesus Christ, who are asleep and resting. You and I are living under Satan's first six thousand years' rule. If we die before the return of Jesus Christ, you and I, will be included with their resurrection.

These include our loved ones who died in our lifetime. Now is the time for them, to have their turn to choose Eternal Life or Eternal death, who are brought up in a resurrection, they are waken up from their long restful sleep, and they will live in a world without Satan, as written in Revelation 20:5 But the rest of the dead did not live again until the thousand years were finished. Revelation 20:12 And I saw the dead, small and great, standing before God, and books were opened. And another book was opened, which is the Book of Life. And the dead were judged according to their works, by the things which were written in the books.

Those resurrected at this time will live one thousand years under the Kingdom of the Living Creator God.

Here is mentioned small and great - babies and old - and that may even include the aborted babies, which were done during the first six thousand years rule under Satan. The babies will grow to become adults during the last one thousand years.

Revelation 20:13 The sea gave up the dead who were in it, and Death and Hades delivered up the dead who were in them.

And they were judged, each one according to his works. God's way of life, as written in the books of the Bible, was revealed to them to be understood, and they will be judged according to how they live in accordance with God's way of life.

All those who died while Satan was ruling this earth for six thousand years will be resurrected into the rule of the Kingdom of God, into God's way of life, without Satan being around. They will resurrect into the Kingdom of God, ruled by Jesus Christ. Their millennium of one thousand years is symbolized by God's annual Great Last Holy Feast day.

I will explain this resurrection, which is with a natural body, of bones, flesh and blood, with a new body like the body we are using during these first six thousand years, from the time of Adam and Eve, as written in Ezekiel 37:1 The hand of the LORD came upon me and brought me out in the Spirit of the LORD, and set me down in the midst of the valley; and it was full of bones.

Ezekiel 37:2 Then He caused me to pass by them all around, and behold, there were very many in the open valley; and indeed they were very dry.

Ezekiel 37:3 And He said to me, "Son of man, can these bones live?" So I answered, "O Lord GOD, You know."

Ezekiel 37:4 Again He said to me, "Prophesy to these bones, and say to them, 'O dry bones, hear the word of the LORD!

Ezekiel 37:5 Thus says the Lord GOD to these bones:

"Surely I will cause breath to enter into you, and you shall live."

Ezekiel 37:6 "I will put sinews on you and bring flesh upon you, cover you with skin and put breath in you; and you shall live. Then you shall know that I *am* the LORD."

Ezekiel 37:7 So I prophesied as I was commanded; and as I prophesied, there was a noise, and suddenly a rattling; and the bones came together, bone to bone.

Ezekiel 37:8 Indeed, as I looked, the sinews and the flesh came upon them, and the skin covered them over; but *there was* no breath in them.

Ezekiel 37:9 Also, He said to me, "Prophesy to the breath, prophesy, son of man, and say to the breath, 'Thus says the Lord GOD: "Come from the four winds, O breath, and breathe on these slain, that they may live."

Ezekiel 37:10 So I prophesied as He commanded me, and breath came into them, and they lived, and stood upon their feet, an exceedingly great army.

Ezekiel 37:11 Then He said to me, "Son of man, these bones are the whole house of Israel. They indeed say, 'Our bones are dry, our hope is lost, and we ourselves are cut off!'

Ezekiel 37:12 Therefore, prophesy and say to them, 'Thus says the Lord GOD: "Behold, O My people, I will open your graves and cause you to come up from your graves, and bring you into the land of Israel."

This last Millennium of one thousand years is represented

by the Last Eight Days of Holy Feast. It starts with a resurrection of all those who lived and died from the time of Adam to the time of Jesus Christ's return from Heaven. This resurrection was known about during the time when Jesus Christ lived, and is also referred to by the last great day as written in John 7:37 . On the last day, that great day of the feast, Jesus stood and cried out, saying, "If anyone thirsts, let him come to Me and drink."

John 6:39 This is the will of the Father who sent Me, that of all He has given Me I should lose nothing, but should raise it up at the last day.

John 6:40 "And this is the will of Him who sent Me, that everyone who sees the Son and believes in Him may have everlasting life; and I will raise him up at the last day."

John 6:44 No one can come to Me unless the Father who sent Me draws him; and I will raise him up at the last day.

John 6:54 Whoever eats My flesh and drinks My blood has eternal life, and I will raise him up at the last day.

We again base these one thousand years, as mentioned earlier, on the concept that one day equals one thousand years, referring to the Living Creator God. As it is referred to as "The Last Great Day", it is also telling us that this millennium of one thousand years is the last millennium in the Living Creator God's plan for mankind.

As mentioned earlier, even Martha knew about this eighth great day resurrection from the dead, when she expected to meet her brother Lazarus again. With a resurrection as written in John 11:24, Martha said to Him, "I know that he will rise again in the resurrection at the last day."

The Last Day of resurrections, comes immediately after the Seven Day Feast of Tabernacles, with no space in between, showing that as soon as judgment on the destruction of Satan, is carried out, and those living who choose eternal life, are changed in a twinkle of an eye, as those who waited for the return of Jesus Christ before them, the eight millennium will start immediately with the resurrection of all those who died captives of Satan.

It is during these last one thousand years that we meet our loved ones who died during our time. We will be able to enjoy their company and their friendship again for one thousand years. We will forget the lost time without them for one thousand years. What a happy time it will be when we meet them again. I am writing for this from the promised Word of God, and it is not my own saying.

Jesus Christ will be in charge of this great resurrection, as written in John 6:39 . This is the will of the Father who sent Me, that of all He has given Me I should lose nothing, but should raise it up at the last day.

John 6:40 And this is the will of Him who sent Me, that everyone who sees the Son and believes in Him may have everlasting life; and I will raise him up at the last day." John 7:37 On the last day, that great day of the feast, Jesus stood and cried out, saying, "If anyone thirsts, let him come to Me and drink."

During the last one thousand years, people will be judged by how they live, as written in John 12:48 . He who rejects Me, and does not receive My words, has that which judges him—the word that I have spoken will judge him in the last day.

Revelation 20:12And I saw the dead, small and great, standing before God, and books were opened. And another book was opened, which is the Book of Life. And the dead were judged according to their works, by the things which were written in the books.

Those living during the last one thousand years will also experience both ways of life. They experienced Satan's way of life during their first life under the ruling of Satan, and now they have resurrected from the dead, into the Kingdom of God, living God's way of life. They will be living the same restful life as those who lived before them, who lived for one thousand years under Jesus Christ, as I have written earlier in this article.

The last thousand years are represented by the eight Holy Feast Days, following the Annual Feast of Tabernacles. It is a Holy Day, which means that the last thousand years will be the same as the seventh thousand years, under the rule of Jesus Christ, with the same benefits.

Now those who are living during this last one thousand years, can make a choice, of either to have an immortal **ETERNAL LIFE** and live forever with the Living Creator God, or to choose the way they lived their first life under Satan, and die their second death, this will be their **ETERNAL DEATH**, never to come back again, as I will explain shortly.

Jesus Christ celebrated the annual Great Last Holy Feast day, as written in John 7:37 . On the last day, that great day of the feast, Jesus stood and cried out, saying, "If anyone thirsts, let him come to Me and drink." Jesus Christ celebrated all the annual Holy Feasts of God, as listed in Leviticus 23."

Those living in these thousand years, and those who choose to live God's way of life, at the end of the one thousand years, they will instantly, at the twinkling of an eye as written earlier, they will receive **ETERNAL LIFE**, changed into spirit beings, and entering into the Family of the Living Creator God, and will live forever. Among those, there will be our loved ones and our friends we knew during our lifetime.

Those who will not choose eternal life will be left standing in their physical bodies, which they were resurrected with.

Now we have the last resurrection from the dead, of those who experienced both ways of life, those who lived during the first one thousand years under Jesus Christ, and deliberately chose death. They will be resurrected in physical bodies; this is their second physical, mortal life. When these are resurrected, they will join those who lived during the eight and last one thousand years, and rejected eternal life, and they are ready to receive their **SECOND DEATH.**

At this time, all those who were in a physical body were thrown into the fire and burned into ashes, never to return again, and will be forgotten forever and ever. This will be their **SECOND DEATH**, as written in Revelation 21:8 "But the cowardly, unbelieving, abominable, murderers, sexually immoral, sorcerers, idolaters, and all liars shall have their part in the lake which burns with fire and brimstone, which is **the SECOND DEATH**."

They would have died twice.

Then Fire will envelop the entire planet Earth and the universe, and dissolve it.

The Living Creator God will dissolve everything and make everything new, as written in 2 Peter 3:11 . Therefore, since all these things will be dissolved, what manner of persons ought you to be in holy conduct and godliness?

2 Peter 3:12 looking for and hastening the coming of the day of God, because of which the heavens will be dissolved, being on fire, and the elements will melt with fervent heat.

2 Peter 3:13 Nevertheless, we, according to His promise, **look for new heavens and a new earth** in which righteousness dwells.

Revelation 21:1 Now I saw a new heaven and a new earth, for **the first heaven and the first earth had passed away.** Also, there was no more sea.

Revelation 21:5 Then He who sat on the throne said, "Behold, I make all things new." And He said to me, "Write, for these words are true and faithful."

Revelation 21:1 Now I saw a new heaven and a new earth, for the first heaven and the first earth had passed away. Also, there was no more sea.

Revelation 21:2 Then I, John, saw the holy city, New Jerusalem, coming down out of heaven from God, prepared as a bride adorned for her husband.

God's dwelling place, and His Throne, will be established here on this planet earth, as written in Revelation 21:3 . And I heard a loud voice from heaven saying, "Behold, the tabernacle of God is with men, and He will dwell with them, and they shall be His people. God Himself will be with them and be their God."

Revelation 21:7 He who overcomes shall inherit all things, and I will be his God and **he shall be My son.**

Now comes the time of the marriage ceremony of Jesus Christ, the Creator, to become the Head of all humanity. This is the marriage ceremony that Jesus Christ mentioned so many times, when He lived as a human being in Jerusalem, as mentioned in Matthew 22:2 : "The kingdom of heaven is like a certain king who arranged a marriage for his son."

Now the Living Creator God is going to move his Habitation in Heaven, and settling it here on this renewed and redesigned Planet, making this planet as it is in Heaven, as we were to pray for this to be done, when Jesus Christ taught us how to pray, as written in, Matthew 6:7 And when you pray, do not use vain repetitions as the heathen do. For they think that they will be heard for their many words.

Matthew 6:8 "Therefore, do not be like them. For your Father knows the things you have need of before you ask Him."

Matthew 6:9 In this manner, therefore, pray: Our Father in heaven, Hallowed be Your name.

Matthew 6:10 **Your kingdom come. Your will be done on earth as it is in heaven.**

God's Throne will be here on this renewed planet as written in Revelation 22:1 . And he showed me a pure river of water of life, clear as crystal, proceeding from the throne of God and of the Lamb.

Revelation 22:2 In the middle of its street, and on either side of the river, was the tree of life, which bore twelve fruits, each tree yielding its fruit every month. The leaves of the tree were for the healing of the nations.

Revelation 22:3 And there shall be no more curse, but the throne of God and of the Lamb shall be in it, and His servants shall serve Him.

It is at this time that the promised marriage Supper takes place, as written in Revelation 19:7 "Let us be glad and rejoice and give Him glory, for the marriage of the Lamb has come, and His wife has made herself ready."

Revelation 19:8 And to her it was granted to be arrayed in fine linen, clean and bright, for the fine linen is the righteous acts of the saints.

Revelation 19:9 Then he said to me, "Write: 'Blessed are

those who are called to the **marriage supper of the Lamb!** " And he said to me, 'These are the true sayings of God."

Now I can confirm what the Apostle Peter wrote, as written in 2 Peter 1:19 . And so we have the prophetic word confirmed, which you do well to heed as a light that shines in a dark place, until the day dawns and the morning star rises in your hearts.

2 Peter 1:20 knowing this first, that no prophecy of Scripture is of any private interpretation,

2 Peter 1:21 for prophecy never came by the will of man, but holy men of God spoke as they were moved by the Holy Spirit.

This is the marriage that Jesus Christ referred to, as written in Matthew 22:1. And Jesus answered and spoke to them again by parables and said:

Matthew 22:2 "The kingdom of heaven is like a certain king who arranged a marriage for his son."

Matthew 22:3 And sent out his servants to call those who were invited to the wedding; and they were not willing to come.

I have already written the following, but I am reiterating it for you in case you have forgotten. Jesus Christ is soon coming down from Heaven, and every eye will see Him coming, as written in Revelation 1:7 Behold, He is coming with clouds, and every eye will see Him, even they who pierced Him. And all the tribes of the earth will mourn because of Him. Even so, Amen.

Revelation 22:6 Then he said to me, "These words are faithful and true." And the Lord God of the holy prophets sent His angel to show His servants the things which must shortly take place.

Revelation 22:7 "Behold, I am coming quickly! Blessed is he who keeps the words of the prophecy of this book."

Revelation 22:12 "And behold, I am coming quickly, and My reward is with Me, to give to everyone according to his work."

Revelation 22:14 Blessed are those who do His commandments, that they may have the right to the tree of life, and may enter through the gates into the city.

The Book of Revelation was written for us to understand it, and it is not sealed, as written in Revelation 22:10 . And he said to me, "Do not seal the words of the prophecy of this book, for the time is at hand."

If you have read this far, I do congratulate you. Now, of what you have read, is out of my boundary. If you believe it or not, it is entirely up to you. I only conveyed to you what has been given to me from above. Keep all this in your mind, and I am sure, that one day in the not too a distant future, you will say **"AHHA"**, George was correct of what he wrote in his article, and you will give thanks to the Living Creator God, and you will realize that you was deceived by Satan, all your lifetime. Satan has deceived the entire world, not just you, as written in Revelation 12:9 . So the great dragon was cast out, that serpent of old, called the Devil and **Satan, who deceives the whole world.**

The results of what is written here in this article are like giving you unripe fruit, which matures with time and is enjoyed when it ripens.

Now it is appropriate to quote to you what the Apostle Peter wrote, in 1 Peter 1:12 To them it was revealed that, not to themselves, but to us they were ministering the things which now have been reported to you, through those who have preached the gospel to you, by the Holy Spirit sent from heaven—**things which angels desire to look into.**

People think and perform many rituals, and do many things, thinking they have the truth, and in fact, they only know Satan, masquerading as Jesus Christ, for the Christians. The real Buddha for the Buddhists, and many other gods around the world. All serving Satan, in many different ways, and they don't know it, thinking they are serving The Living Creator God, as written in John 16:2 . They will put you out of the synagogues; yes, the time is coming that **whoever kills you, will think that he offers God service.**

This is the reason why the Living Creator God has a salvation plan, for every human being on earth, a plan of eight thousand years, as I have written in this short article.

No matter what colour, or what shade of your skin, you come under, the Living Creator God have predestinated and included you in His plan, even before He created the Universe. **The Living Creator God knew you, from before He even**

198

created the universe, as written in Romans 8:29: For whom He foreknew, He also predestined to be conformed to the image of His Son, that He might be the firstborn among many brethren.

Romans 8:30 Moreover, whom **He predestined**, these He also called; whom He called, these He also justified; and whom He justified, these He also glorified.

Ephesians 1:4 Just as **He chose us in Him before the foundation of the world**, that we should be holy and without blame before Him in love.

Ephesians 1:5 Having **predestined us** to adoption as sons by Jesus Christ to Himself, according to the good pleasure of His will.

Ephesians 1:11 In Him also we have obtained an inheritance, **being predestined** according to the purpose of Him who works all things according to the counsel of His will.

I don't ask for any credits, I wrote this article on behalf of my Father in Heaven, Who gave me His Spirit, like He did with His Son Jesus Christ, and may my Father in Heaven, bless everyone whom He chooses, as written in John 6:44 No one can come to Me unless the Father who sent Me draws him; and I will raise him up at the last day.

It is the living Creator God the Father, who is choosing and calling out from Satan's kingdom, the ones He wants at this time, to be kings in the coming Kingdom of God. The rest are not lost, but they will have their turn when Satan is gone.

Revelation 22:20 He who testifies to these things says, **"Surely I am coming quickly." Amen. Even so, come, Lord Jesus!**

Revelation 22:21 The grace of our Lord Jesus Christ be with you all. Amen.

www.ingramcontent.com/pod-product-compliance
Lightning Source LLC
Chambersburg PA
CBHW040844120626
46547CB00001B/13